CONTENTS

GW01459821

＊＊

ACKNOWLEDGEMENTS

Grateful thanks to the following people for their help in this guide:-

Andy Norfolk for section artwork, headings & computer alignments.
Ian Cooke for plan of Halligye fogou.
Craig Weatherhill for plan of Nine Maidens, Wendron stone circle.
Andrew Langdon for some information on crosses.
Cornwall Archaeological Unit for some information on sites.
Charles Thomas & Carl Thorpe for drawing of Carnsew inscribed stone.

Text and artwork copyright Meyn Mamvro publications and may not be reproduced with permission. Correspondence on any aspect of this booklet is welcomed and should be sent to: Meyn Mamvro, 51 Carn Bosavern, St Just, Penzance, Cornwall TR19 7QX.

All years are expressed in the non-denominational format: BCE (Before Current Era) = B.C, CE (Current Era) = A.D.

1

Introduction

This booklet is the 3rd in the series of Earth Mysteries Guides for Cornwall, following on from the ones on West Penwith and Bodmin Moor and North Cornwall (including Tintagel). This 3rd Guide completes the coverage of mainland Cornwall, and covers a large diffuse area from the borders of West Penwith to the borders of Devon. It is sub-divided into 4 main sections: firstly, the area of west Cornwall stretching from West Penwith to a line joining Falmouth with St.Agnes; secondly, The Lizard, that separate area to the south of Helston; thirdly, Mid Cornwall, the heart of Cornwall running to the Saints Way line that joins Padstow to Fowey; and fourthly, South-East Cornwall, the area south of Bodmin Moor that runs to the Tamar boundary. Within these four areas there is a tremendous diversity of sites, not concentrated in one specific area like West Penwith or Bodmin Moor. Instead there are clusters of sites around granitic uplands like Carn Brea, Carnmenellis, St.Austell Downs, St.Breock Downs, Kit Hill etc, and isolated stones, crosses, and wells in what are often remote and secluded places.

The booklet takes you on a journey from almost one end of Cornwall to the other, and along the way points to the principal sites and places worth visiting in each area. It is the first and only Guide to incorporate Earth Mysteries information, that area of research that covers alignments, anomalous phenomena, folklore and legend, a way of trying to interpret the past that provides an insight into the mindset of the people who built them. As well as the large geographical area covered by the booklet (about 80 miles in length), the sites chosen cover a long extent of time: the Mesolithic (6000-4000 BCE), the Neolithic (4000-2500 BCE), Bronze Age (2500-600 BCE), Iron Age/Celtic (600 BCE-500 CE) and early Christian (500-900 CE). Each area has at least one location map, and all sites are given 8 or 6 figure grid references. Most locations are identifiable from the 1:50,000 O.S maps [203 covering west Cornwall and west Lizard; 204 covering east Lizard and Truro & Falmouth areas; 200 covering Newquay & St.Austell areas; and 201 covering SE Cornwall], but for accurate location of specific sites in particular areas the 1:25,000 Pathfinder maps are invaluable. Whichever may you chose to visit the sites, may this Booklet guide and help you to find and enjoy these very special places from Cornwall's past.

Cheryl Straffon
Samhain, 1994.

west cornwall

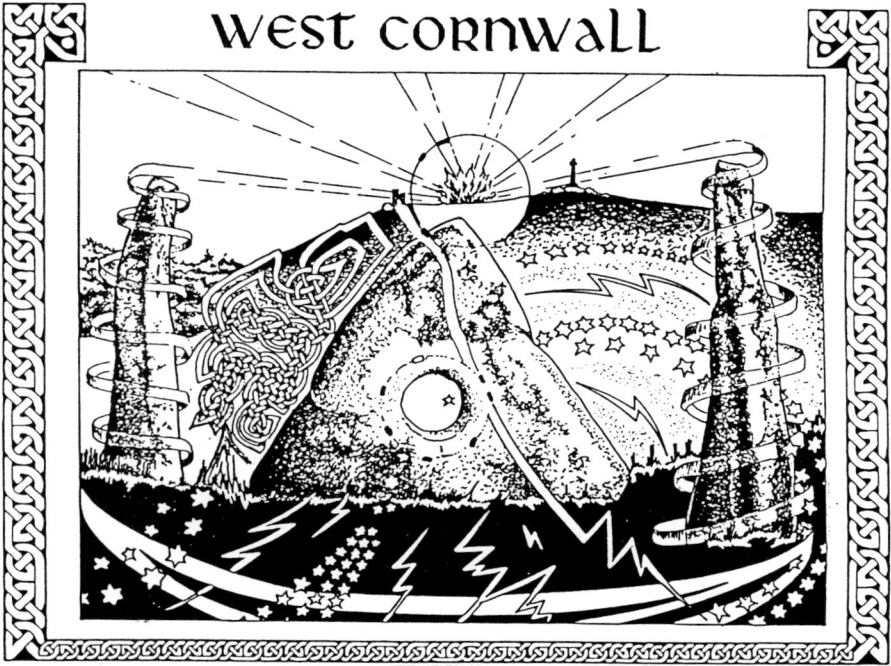

At the borders of West Penwith, west Cornwall continues to a line running roughly from Penryn/Falmouth in the south to St.Agnes in the north. This is a land scarred in the northern half by the heavily-industrial mining remains of the 18th & 19th centuries, a world many miles away from the pretty seaside villages and quaint fishing harbours so beloved by the Tourist industry. But this land is occupied by the Cornish people who have to make a hard living from meagre resources, and it was occupied too in the past by those who have left their remnants in the landscape. For amongst the mining chimneys and workaday towns, there lie pockets of ancient sites, stone circles, standing stones, quoits, wells, and crosses, often focused around the number of holy hilltops in the area, hills that were revered and celebrated by our ancestors as being of the body of Mother Earth. We may have since torn the heart out of that body, but the ancient sites remain to remind us that once the land was cared for and not exploited en masse, and once people were in touch with the sacredness of it.

In the southern half of the area, the land becomes softer, and the sites often hidden away on farms and in wooded glades. Here there are standing stones, a holed stone, a fogou, wells and crosses, dotted about over the landscape, many not well-known or visited. Here there is the pleasure of discovering a site all to oneself, and of trying to see it and the surrounding land through the eyes of our ancestors who placed it there for a specific purpose, still known only to them. We may look at its alignments, dowse its energies, investigate its properties, but many of these sites still keep their secrets today. These lesser-known sites need as much care, if not more, than the more famous Cornish monuments, and continuing to visit them helps protect them and pay homage to their special qualities.

TRENCROM HILL (SW5177 3620)

A line drawn from St.Ives Island on the north coast to St.Michael's Mount on the south bisects Trencrom Castle, a Neolithic hill fort. The fort, or to be more precise, tor enclosure, follows the countours of the hill summit itself, making an irregular pear-shaped structure. The walls, which may date from the later Iron Age, are 15ft thick in places, and two distinctive gateway stones survive. There were originally a large number of hut circles inside, perhaps as many as 16.

There are also wells at the settlement, one up a hidden path at the north end of the tor, one on the eastern slope known as Giant's Well (SW520 363). The Giant in question was called Trecobben, who would sling his hammer across to Cormoran, the Giant of St.Michael's Mount, a legend that may be a memory of the geomantic 'ley' line running across the land between the sites.

On the NE flanks of the hill lie 2 interesting stones. One is a menhir called **Beersheba** (SW5251 3714), a fine 10½ft standing stone. A line from the hill through the stone continued NE also runs through the **Longstone** at Carbis Bay (SW5303 3821).

The other stone is a huge boulder known as **The Bowl Rock** (SW5220 3642), its legend to do with the Giants who bowled enormous stones down the hill and across the land to mark out their territory. Again, there is memory of the ancient geomantic marking of the land.

<u>CARN BREA</u> (SW6860 4059)

Some 12 miles further up from Trencrom Hill lies a very similar Neolithic <u>hill fort</u>. Carn Brea, some 735ft <u>high,</u> towers over the land hereabouts littered with old mine workings. Like Trencrom, greenstone axes were found here, showing occupation as early as 3900 BCE. Prehistoric fortifications enclose the twin-peaked summit, and the 200 or so inhabitants lived a peaceful life for about 300 years before the site was attacked and burnt.

Like Trencrom, there is a <u>well</u> lying below the large northern rampart, covered by an ancient <u>structure</u> of granite and reputed never to run dry. There is also legend of a <u>secret tunnel</u> from the Castle to St.Euny Church, which are often folkloric <u>memories</u> of ancient earth currents or ley lines. At the SW base of the hill in a field are 2 <u>standing stones</u>, each about 5ft high, pointing in a direct N-S direction towards <u>a rocky outcrop</u> on the hill. A midsummer sunrise <u>alignment</u> has also been identified from a 15ft standing stone on the SE side <u>of the</u> fort. At sunrise on midsummer morning, a back-shadow runs from a stone stump (twin of the stone?) to the stone and back to a line of gatepost stones leading into the fort. Truly a hill of the sun.

Also like Trencrom, there is a legend of the <u>Giant</u> of the hill, who feuded with the <u>Giant</u> Bolster of St. Agnes Beacon (SW7100 5025), some 6 miles to the north. These two giants would often hurl boulders across the space between the two hills, and Bolster was able to stride from the Beacon to Carn Brea with one mighty step. Bolster has an <u>earth bank</u> named after him that <u>originally ran</u> for some 2 miles enclosing St. Agnes Beacon, and the Carn Brea giant has several natural <u>rocks</u> named after him on the hill, <u>such</u> as The Giant's Head, Hand, Couch, & Cradle. All this shows that the giants were seen to be very much alive in the land, and may be a distant folk memory of ancient gods and goddesses. Another giant nearby on the coast at Portreath was called Wrath, which may be from the Cornish (g)rath = witch, hag, or crone.

5

CARNMENELLIS

S & E of Carn Brea and visible from it are several other holy hilltops, each of which have ancient barrows on them. About 3 miles to the east is Carn Marth; about a mile SE is the hilltop of Carnkie, crowned by the Pillamine Barrows; another mile further S is Gregwartha (near Fourlanes); and another couple of miles S the hilltop of Carnmenellis, which at 820ft high, surpasses even Carn Brea. Carnmenellis is the focus for a number of ancient sites, a megalithic complex, that lie around its flanks and fields.

NINE MAIDENS STONE CIRCLE

(SW6831 3653) About a mile W of Carnmenellis and close to the B3267 road from Redruth to Helston, the twin hills of Carnmenellis and Carn Brea are very much in sight from the circle. The circle seems to be specifically aligned to an outcrop on Carnmenellis summit denoting the equinox sunrise, and there may also be a midwinter sunset alignment to Crowan Beacon, about 1½ miles SW.

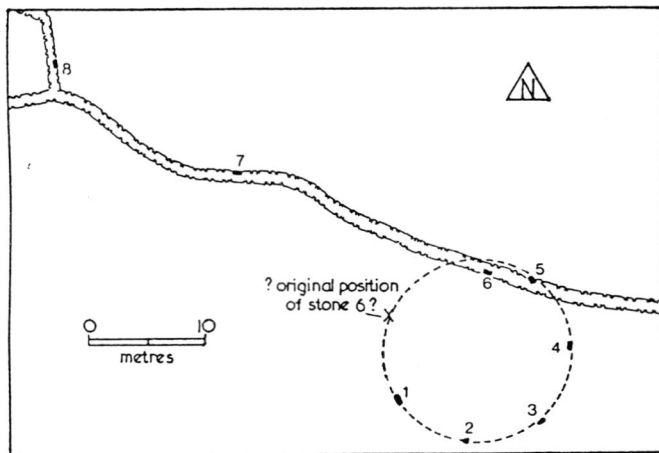

There were formerly 2 circles here, but now part of only one (the SE) remains, with 6 stones standing including 2 in a dividing wall. The 2nd circle to the NW a few yards away at SW6829 3656 is now destroyed, but 2 stones (nos. 7 & 8 on the drawing) remain in situ in the wall.

There was also a standing stone nearby at CALVADNACK (SW 6898 3552), now lying prostrate and half buried in a field.

To the north of Carnmenillis at FOUR LANES there was formerly a possible stone row (SW6865 3940), and a holed stone at MENAGISSEY (SW7126 4673).

About ½ mile to the W of the Nine Maidens stone circle stands a round barrow called **Hangman's Barrow** (SW6737 3669), a massive ruined cairn over 9ft high and 65ft in diameter. There is no record of the tomb's contents, but presumably it must have been the main burial chamber of the people who built the stone circle. Another 1½ miles to the NW lies another kind of burial chamber, a dolmen called **Carwynnen Quoit** (SW6500 3720).

This now lies in a ruined condition in a private field, but is in the process of being restored. Before the chamber collapsed (in 1967) it had 3 uprights (of 4½ft or so) with the 11¼ft x 8ft capstone on top. Unusually it lies in a valley, whereas other quoits elsewhere generally lie on high ground.

To the S of the Nine Maidens stone circle lie 2 standing stones. **Burras** (SW6795 3445) is a 10ft high menhir in a field next to a farmhouse, again just off the B3297 road. It was re-erected in the early 1900s in a large pit, by the Pearse brothers with a steam engine, and it is now set in concrete. Carnmenellis hilltop lies NE of the standing stone, indicating a summer solstice sunrise alignment.

Prospidnick (SW6592 3155), also known as The Long-stone, is also about 10ft high and stands in a hedge at a bend on a minor road at the base of Prospidnick Hill, about 2½ miles SW of Burras menhir. It aligns with Burras towards Carnmenellis Hill, and also with the Hangman's Barrows towards Carn Brea Hill. There was formerly another standing stone nearby at ap. 635318.

7

STITHIANS AREA

A few miles to the east of Cammenellis is the Stithians area. A large part of the area is taken up with the Stithians reservoir, and here a very curious discovery was made in the summer droughts of 1984, 1989 & 1990. When the water line dropped very low 10 cup-marked stones were uncovered (at SW7171 3536) all with multiple cup marks, one stone having broken into three, making 12 stones in all. One stone (the broken one) was decorated with at least 48 cupmarks, but some of the others had only half a dozen or so. On most of the stones the arrangement of the cupmarks seems to be quite random, but on others, particularly the flat slabs, it is possible to see some degree of organisation in the form of of straight lines, arcs and circles. The size of the cupmarks is similar to those on Tregiffian Barrow in West Penwith, and it has been suggested that these could represent a local version of the Bronze-Age cup markings already noted in other parts of Britain – a special Cornish version of such rock-art. It is a small irony that our era has seen fit to submerge them beneath the waters, in a way not dissimilar to the Bronze Age custom of giving sacred objects to the goddesses of rivers and seas!

To the east of the reservoir is another standing stone. Tremenhere (SW7485 3672) lies beside a farm on the minor road from Stithians to Burnthouse. It is a finely-tapering 9ft high stone, lying almost due east from Cammenellis hill, indicating an equinoxical sunset to the hill, and on a direct line to a possible former standing stone at Carnsidga (SW7264 3655) and on to the Nine Maidens stone circle.

Nearby there were formerly 2 other possible stone circles at Carncress (SW7228 3628) and Goonorman (SW7495 3569), and a menhir at Crosspost Farm (SW7447 3838).

CONSTANTINE AREA

Moving south from Stithians, there are a number of interesting and original sites in the low-lying Constantine area, near the Helford estuary. Here at Maen Pern once stood a 24ft menhir, the tallest standing stone in Cornwall until it was broken up in the mid–18thC. 250 years later two more extant standing stones illustrate the Christian response to these pagan sites.

At **Mabe Churchyard** (SW7573 3245) there is a 6ft standing stone in the churchyard itself amongst the gravestones. It has been Christianised with a Latin cross carved on to the N face near the top, indicating that the church was built around an original pagan site, and the stone incorporated into the churchyard.

A mile further south off the B3291 from Penryn to Gweek at Higher Eathorne Farm lies another standing stone, the now infamous **Eathorne** menhir (SW7460 3134). This fine curved 8ft stone stood here for some 4000 years before being ripped out by farmer Philip Clemoes in 1992 and dumped in the hedge.

Clemoes was a born–again Christian who feared the stone could be used for "pagan practices". He intended to break up the stone, and in fact during the uprooting had already broken off the top, but pressure from the archaeologists and an outcry by the local Earth Mysteries Group forced him to think again. In 1993 the stone was replaced in the same field, but, because English Heritage would not fund an excavation, it was re-erected in a different place 15 yards from its original position nearer the hedge, thus destroying the context or setting of the site, and making the research into landscape patterns more difficult. The whole saga was a sad and sorry tale of unnecessary vandalism.

9

Two other interesting sites lie in the same area. About a mile further S towards Gweek at Trewardreva, also in a field beside the road is **Piskey Hall** fogou (SW7280 3003). This is a small fogou with a slightly curved passage some 26½ft long, once part of a now-destroyed Iron Age settlement. It is somewhat different to other fogous [see p21], being only partly-underground, vertical walls (not corbelled) covered with 8 huge roof-slabs, and no obvious creep or side-passages. It is however aligned NE-SW to the midsummer sunrise, as are most other fogous, and indicates a ritual use for the structure.

A couple of miles further on the road leads into Gweek, and beside a minor road leading due N about a mile from the village is Tolvan Cross. In the back garden of the cottage (seek permission to view) lies a unique monument the **Tolvan Stone** (SW7063 2770) This is a large triangular slab 7½ft high x 7ft base which contains a circular hole in the centre 1½ft in diameter, large enough for a child to get through

It was at one time moved across the road but later moved back. A barrow formerly stood nearby and it may have come from that: barrows with entrance stones with holes are known from elsewhere, but if so it would have been a large structure. Legends of healing became attached to the stone and by as late as 1880 mothers would bring their infirm children to the site to pass them through the holed stone.

10

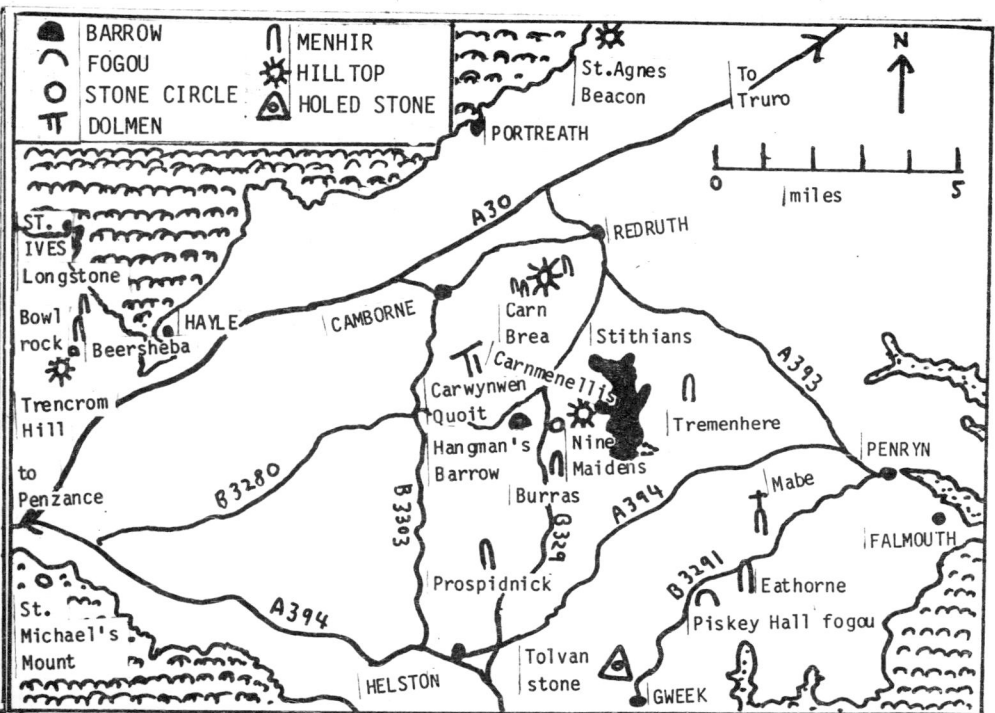

Legend (top map):
- ◗ BARROW
- ◠ FOGOU
- ○ STONE CIRCLE
- ⊓ DOLMEN
- ⋂ MENHIR
- ☼ HILL TOP
- △ HOLED STONE

St.Agnes Beacon
To Truro
PORTREATH
0 miles 5
N

A30
REDRUTH

ST. IVES
Longstone
Bowl rock
HAYLE
Beersheba
CAMBORNE
A393

Carn Brea
Stithians
Carnmenellis
Carwynwen Quoit
Tremenhere
Hangman's Barrow
Nine Maidens
PENRYN
Mabe
FALMOUTH

Trencrom Hill
to Penzance
B3280
B3303
B3329
Burras
A394
B3291
Eathorne
Piskey Hall fogou

St. Michael's Mount
A394
Prospidnick
HELSTON
Tolvan stone
GWEEK

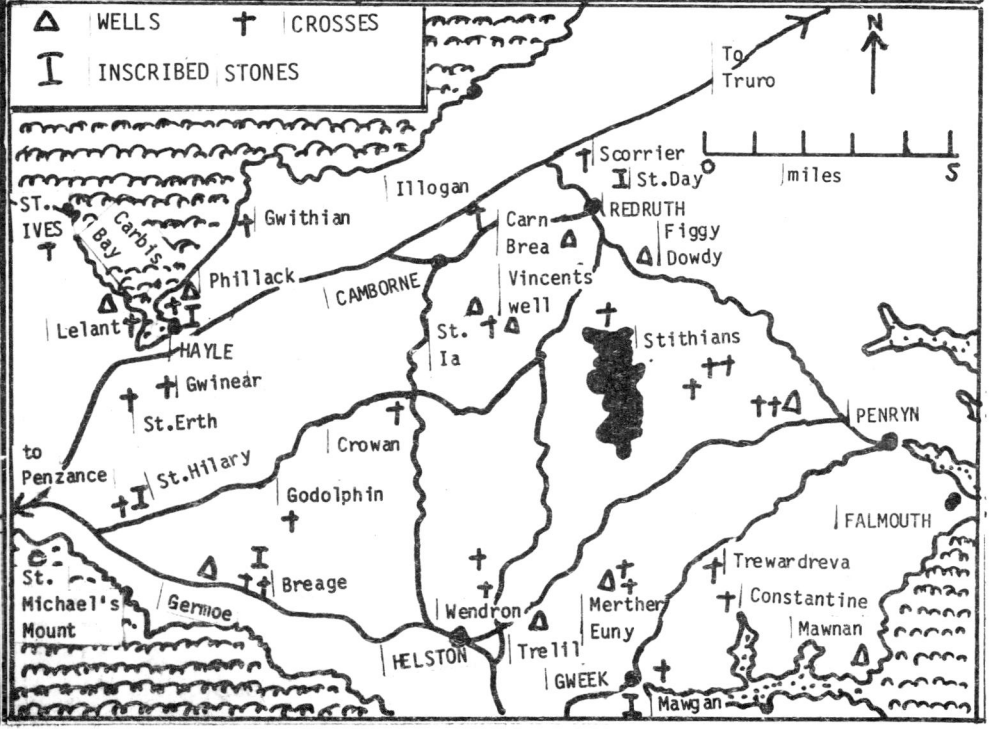

Legend (bottom map):
- △ WELLS
- ✝ CROSSES
- I INSCRIBED STONES

To Truro
N
Scorrier
St.Day
0 miles 5

ST. IVES
Carbis Bay
Gwithian
Illogan
Carn Brea
REDRUTH
Figgy Dowdy
Vincents well
CAMBORNE

Lelant
Phillack
HAYLE
St. Ia
Stithians
PENRYN

Gwinear
St.Erth
Crowan
FALMOUTH

to Penzance
St.Hilary
Godolphin
Trewardreva
Constantine
Mawnan

St. Michael's Mount
Germoe
Breage
Wendron
Merther Euny
Trelil
HELSTON
GWEEK
Mawgan

LELANT – St.Euny's Well (SW536 387). Reached from the end of Headland Rd at Carbis Bay, where a track goes down across the railway line and through a beautiful nut grove with stunning views across the bay. The well is an enchanting pool issuing from a low rock fissure and tumbling down to the coast below. Famed as a Fairy Well or wishing well, some cloths have been tied to a tree above. ↓

Fenton Sauras well (SW542 369). lies in a private house (the Abbey). It has an imposing stone structure though is now overgrown.

HAYLE – Phillack Well (SW565 384). Situated across the road from Phillack Church on a piece of waste ground, this well has no stone surround but is a hole in the ground. It was profaned in 1720 by Erasmus Pascoe, Sherriff of Cornwall, who washed his mangy dog in it, he and his son then dying a dreadful death. The well has recently (1993) been restored by Hayle Old Cornwall Society.

GERMOE – St.Germoe's Well (SW584 294). At Germoe off the Penzance-Helston road. It is in a pretty setting, but the well was restored not very tastefully in 1979 with an iron grid over the structure.

TROON – St.Ia's Well (SW658 383) This well rises in the chapel of St.Ia (sister of Euny and patron saint of St.Ives) which lies in a beautiful wooded gorge ½mile west of the village. However, the farmer of Chytodden unfortunately does not allow access to it through his land.

CARN BREA – St.Euny's Well (SW691 413). Mentioned on p.5, this well lies beside a stream in the small village at the bottom of Carn Brea hill, opposite the Village Hall. A pretty setting, though the well could do with being cleaned out. ↓

GWENNAP – Figgy Dowdy's Well (SW715 406). This lies in the back garden of Rocky Field house on the south side of Carn Marth, once a holy hilltop with barrows. It is now overgrown though the well structure with beehive roof is intact. There is an old rhyme about Figgy Dowdy (who may originally have been a harvest Goddess) keeping the well locked less people should take her water away.

FOUR LANES – Vincents Well (SW676 377). A healing well with a reputation for curing eyes. It is not the Shute in Bolenowe hamlet (given in Meyrick's Guide to Holy Wells) but is a spring under some granite slabs up an overgrown lane in a marshy area, accessible from Forest Farm. On 2½" OS map but difficult to find.

WENDRON (Trelil) – St.Wendronas Well (SW677 285). On the south side of the A394 Helston–Penryn road (park in layby at top of hill). Excellently preserved well-building with seats inside and clear running stream. Legend of the attempt to build a church here, which was frustrated by crows (pagan symbols) who removed the stones every night, indicating powerful pagan site. A track from the layby leads to Tremenheere Farm, but no trace or memory now of any standing stone there. ↓

Merther Euny Well (SW704 295). A couple of miles further along the A394 at Trevenen a turning leads to the farm of Merther Euny. From here, a track leads down into the woods and after 100 yds the well is below the bank on the right. An enchanting spot with the sound of the river tumbling below. ↓

STITHIANS – Lady Holy Well (SW750 376). From Kennal Farm a public footpath runs for a mile NE, and the well lies in a wooded copse above the Kennal Vale, surrounded by holly trees. The water flows from the hillside into a granite trough and basin, which is however unfortunately beside some rusting corrogated iron which needs clearing up. Nevertheless a very beautiful and secluded spot. ↓

MAWNAN – (SW787 273). This singular well lies in the grounds of the Old Rectory house on the right of a bend just before Mawnan church. Reached by a hidden path leading down a ravine, the imposing well with beautiful clear water is built into the side of the overhang. It has a "Celtic" head carved above the entrance. A mysterious place. ↓

13

HALSETOWN [Nr.St.Ives] (SW5047 3880). A round-headed cross on granite base stands on a low hedge beside the B3311 road. Nearby at PENBEAGLE (SW5079 3987) at the junction of the B3306 a roughly-cut cross with a small incised cross stands against a wall.

LELANT. A number of ancient Celtic crosses here. In the churchyard (SW5486 3772) overlooking the Hayle estuary there are 2. One is a round-headed cross beside the south side of the church, which originally came from Trevethow, and was moved to the top of Trencrom Hill in 1907 where its head was broken off by miners. It was subsequently replaced, and returned to Trevethow, finally coming to rest at Lelant church-yard. The second is a tall round-headed cross near the trees. ↓

In Lelant cemetery (SW5477 3773) there are 3 other ancient crosses and numerous modern copies. In Lelant Lane (SW5416 3788) a cross was re-discovered and re-erected in 1956. In Lelant Sea Lane (SW5421 3661) beside the A3074 road a round-headed cross with incised Latin cross stands on a prominent hedge wall.

PHILLACK CHURCHYARD (nr.Hayle) (SW5651 3838). A very early site, indicated by the Chi-Rho symbol above the church porch. In the churchyard is an inscribed stone [see p.17], beside which is a wheel-headed cross. And opposite the lychgate is a cross with a decorated shaft and a four-holed beaded head on the back of which are five raised bosses. Opposite the churc' is the ancient holy well [see p.12]. ↙

PHILLACK MEXICO CROSS (SW5625 3850). A short distance past the church a rough lane on the right leads to Mexico Towans. A horse-shoe-shaped headed cross made of Pentewan stone stands in the hedge of a field on the left.

GWITHIAN CHURCHYARD (SW5866 4126) A round-headed cross with an equal-limbed cross carved within.

GWINEAR CHURCHYARD (SW5952 3737). A large weathered cross stands beside a pathway in the churchyard. It formerly stood at a crossroads about $3/4$ miles to the east. GWINEAR POLMENOR (SW6187 3865). Near the railway lane along a lane this is a wide-limbed Latin cross.

ST.ERTH CHURCHYARD (SW5497 3501). A large four-holed cross with deeply-sculptured figure, on the back of which are 5 bosses.

ST. HILARY CHURCHYARD (SW5500 3126). Two crosses here, both beside the path. Both have raised Latin crosses, one well proportioned within a wheel-head.

BREAGE. Two small crosses here, one outside a nursery at Trevena (SW6129 2843) and the other, which is uniquely made of sandstone, in the churchyard (SW6185 2843). Langdon suggested that the ornament on the shaft resembled a dragon's head.

GODOLPHIN CHURCHYARD (SW6088 3131). A 6'6" equi-limbed incised cross formerly used as a gatepost at Chytodden. The original sites of this and another cross at Spernon (SW6086 3130) would have been in direct line between Godolphin & Breage parish churches.

CLOWANCE ESTATE, CROWAN. Three crosses stand in the grounds of this holiday timeshare estate.
1](SW6352 3476) originally from Boldgate crossroads is on a wooded island in the middle of a lake (but not visible from the shore)
2](SW6370 3537) originally from Binnerton crossroads is in a bluebell wood to the N of the park.
3](SW6337 3486) originally from Nine Maidens Downs was re-erected in 1990 to the SW of the park.

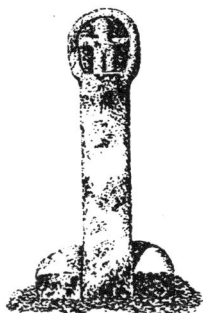

TRESLOTHAN CHURCH (SW6504 3780). A small (2'7") well preserved cross originally from the Pendarves estate It has a curiously carved Christ figure with legs akimbo!

ILLOGAN CHURCHYARD (SW6667 4183). A 5' cross, probably standing in situ. The shaft goes down into the ground for at least another 5ft. It has a square cross on one side and a diagonal on the other.

SCORRIER HOUSE. On private estate. 1](SW7240 4370) 4'10" Ting Tang or White Cross. 2](SW7243 4372) is a 6½' ornamented cross which formerly stood on the Helston-Penryn road.

STITHIANS. 6 crosses in this area. 1](SW7312 3714) 6' wheel-headed cross in churchyard formerly from Reppers Mill, ½mile further E. 2](SW7310 3715) 3'10" cross with 4 sinkings now in Vicarage garden. 3](SW7099 3798) A small cross-head found in 1955 and now on a garden wall at Penhalvean to the NW. 4](SW7294 3613) 4' cross found in 1921 in bed of river and now on bend in road at Tretheague Mill. 5](SW7443 3582) 7' cross with carvings on both sides in farmhouse field at Trevalis 2½ miles to SW. 6](SW7408 3614) 6'2" cross standing in field also at Trevalis, with a very interesting carving of a female-style figure above a heart.↓

Binnerton cross

15

WENDRON. In the Wendron area are two crosses with checkered histories. One (SW6790 3101) formerly stood at the Manhay/Trevennan crossroads before being removed, split in two and built into a hedge. In 1887 it was recovered and remounted, but then thrown down again. It then went to the Manhay-vean farmyard before being removed to Wendron cemetery (SW6790 3101).

A mile or so to the NW by the roadside at Bodilly (SW6693 3225) is a cross that formerly stood on the crest of Farms Common hill and was known as the "Wendron God". [Illustrated below] It has also been thrown down and apppropriated a number of times. It seems that the inhabitatants of Wendron parish had no great reverence for their Cornish crosses! ↓

TREVEASE (SW7251 3150). A 4'10" high nicely-carved cross next to a footpath from Trevease farm, off the Helston-Penryn road. It could have indicated where the old churchpath made a safe crossing place across the stream.

TREWARDREVA (SW7280 3022). A 7'9" cross with incised lines, standing where ancients roads meet, near to Pixie's Hall fogou [see p.10]. It had fallen and was re-erected in in 1865.

MERTHER EUNY. Two crosses here. One (SW7019 2912) is a 6'2" cross standing beside the road on Polglaze Hill, with a tradition of a man buried below it. The other (SW7030 2932) stands in a hedge near the old Chapel above Merther Euny well [see p.13]. It is 5'6" in height and covered with most unusual ornamentation. ↓

NANJARROW, Constantine (SW7353 2970). This 2'10" inscribed cross may have been the original churchway cross. It is now set up on a hedge in a farm with several feet of the shaft buried.

BONALLACK, Nr Gweek (SW7190 2645). This beautiful and unusual 4'5" cross formerly stood by the side of the path leading to Trelil holy well [see p.13]. It was then moved to a garden in Helston, before its present location. There is a double chevron carved on it with horseshoes added on the front and back, perhaps by the Ferrers (Farriers) family who owned property near the holy well.

16

CARNSEW nr Hayle (SW5564 3716). This inscribed stone is cemented into the upper walk of the small park by the W end of the Hayle viaduct, most of the park being formed out of a little Iron Age fort. The stone is badly-worn and has been broken and joined together. It reads HIC PA CE NUP REQVIEVIT CVNAIDE HIC IN TVMVLO IACIT VIXIT ANNOS XXX III = "Here in peace lately went to rest Cunaide. Here in the grave she lies. She lived 33 years". Cunaide is an Irish name and the stone probably dates from the 5thC.

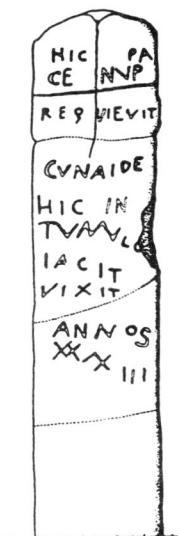

Drawing [c] Charles Thomas & Carl Thorpe first published in "Meyn Mamvro" no.19.

PHILLACK CHURCH (SW5635 3841). Above the south-porch door is an early chi-rho stone, containing the 2 Greek letters X & P, the first letters of CHRISTOS. In the CHURCHYARD (SW5655 3842) standing against a wall, next to a cross, is an inscribed stone with the letters CLOTVALI MOBRATTI = "(The grave of) Clotualus, (son of) Mobrattus".

ST.HILARY CHURCH (SW5503 3127). In the church there is a 4thC (306-8) Roman milestone with 10 lines of inscription referring to the emperor Constantine In the churchyard there is a small inscribed stone NOTI NOTI = "Notus, son of Notus".

BREAGE CHURCH (SW6180 2850). A 3rdC (258-268) Roman markstone dedicated to the emperor Postumus.

MAWGAN CROSS (SW7071 2486). This headless 10thC cross-shaft stands in the centre of the village on the road to Halligye fogou [see p.21]. 6ft high inscribed CNEGVMI FILI GENAIVS="Cnegumus, son of Genaius".

MENHEER FARM, St.Day (SW7199 4218). This 3rdC (238-244) Roman milestone dedicated to emperor Antonius Gordianus was discovered during ploughing in 1942 and now stands in the farmhouse garden.

There was formerly an inscribed stone in St.Euny's Church, Redruth, noted by Borlase in 1740, reading MAVOVIH VITO = "Mavorius (son of) Victor" (?) but destroyed in 1768.

17

the Lizard

The Lizard is a secret land. Unlike the concentration of sites in particular areas in the rest of Cornwall, the Lizard has few obvious centres of antiquity, but rather a scattering of individual places of sanctity. A standing stone here, a fogou there, one well here, one cross there, hidden, private, secluded. The Lizard does not reveal her secrets easily. She has many different faces for different people: the strangeness of her rock formations; the downs of Goonhilly dominated by a futuristic communications dish complex, a wind farm – and a remote standing stone; a network of lanes – beautiful in springtime – seeming to lead nowhere, but then opening up into a well or fogou site; isolated churches containing hidden secrets; old tracks dating back into pre-history leading down to the coast. A land of much mystery and strangeness that only communicates itself slowly and gradually, and takes a long while to begin to understand.

The area has an ancient tradition of quiet spirituality. A land set-apart, a sense of something more, behind or beyond or beneath things visible or tangible. An atmosphere of enchantment, almost a living presence of spiritual power. It is a place to "dream dreams and see visions", and ancient and modern mystics have been irresistibly drawn to the area. Here, hidden from public view, can be found shamanic cults that connect with with the Serpent Goddess of the land, pellars with their ancient wisdom of spellcraft, geomancers following the twisting energy spirals, and seekers after the mystery and the meaning of the sacred sites. These sites are best visited in ones and twos and threes, places to deeply connect with the earth spirit, to perhaps sit and meditate awhile, perhaps even in an altered state of consciousness. The magic of the Lizard runs very deep: go and seek for it, but be careful what you find!

HALLIGYE FOGOU

(SW7132 2395). Most fogous (underground chambers dating from the Iron Age) are confined to West Penwith: this exception is a spectacular site in the grounds of Trelowarren estate (signposted from the drive). It formerly stood within an Iron Age settlement but is now in a beautifully maintained enclosure.

It consists of a long entrance passage [e], leading into a lower passage accessible only on hands and knees [h], which was the original entrance [j]. Leading off to the left is another curving passage [b], some 55ft long, at the end of which is a small inner chamber [f], which may have been used for ritual purposes to connect with the womb of Mother Earth. This curved passage is orientated to NE in the direction of the midsummer sunrise. Altogether there is a total of some 126ft of passage with corbelled walls and a roof of heavy slabs. Some psychic experiences have been reported at this fogou, as with some others, and a Cornish Earth Mysteries Group imaging session with about 30 people meditating in the darkness produced some fascinating parallel imagery around shamanistic flight.

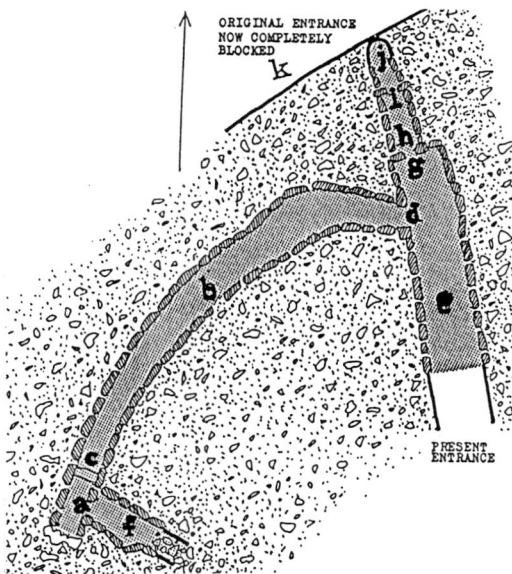

a. DOORWAY - 2'1"high, 1'9"wide.
b. MAIN PASSAGE - 55'long, 6'high, 4'wide.
c. STUMBLING BLOCK - 2'high, 1'6"wide.
d. DOORWAY - 3'5"high, 2'4"wide.
e. SECOND PASSAGE - 28'long, 5'6"wide, 6'high.
f. INNER CHAMBER - 10'long, 3'wide, 3'6"high.
g. DOORWAY - 2'3"high, 1'5"wide.
h. INNER CREEP PASSAGE - 6'6"long, 2'3"wide, 3'high.
i. DOORWAY - 2'6"high, 1'4"wide.
j. OUTER CREEP PASSAGE - 6'long, 2'wide, 2'6"high.
k. POSITION OF DITCH - now filled in.

STANDING STONES

There are a number of standing stones in the Lizard, which are not in alignment to each other, but do align to other significant sites.

Drytree (SW7256 2119) lies just off the B3293 St.Keverne road behind the Goonhilly Downs satellite station with its great dish aerials. It is an impressive 9ft menhir, re-erected in 1928. A number of alignments run from it (see p.23) and also a line from it running to Chynhalls Point cliff-castle goes through Trelanvean Cross (see p.21), perhaps marking a now-forgotten ley-path.

Crousa Common (SW7752 2009) is a double-stone site (one fallen) lying in a marshy field to the N of the B3293 where it divides to Coverack and St.Keverne. The stone still standing is about 6' tall, and an alignment runs from the stones through the Three Brothers of Grugith (see p.21) to the aforementioned Trelanvean Cross. The site also stands on a line between Nare Point headland to the NE and Poldowrian cliff castle to the SW (see p.21).

Tremenhir (SW7777 2103) is a large 10ft menhir near St.Keverne in a field next to a trackway leading from the farm named after the stone. It aligns with the aforementioned Trelanvean Cross and a group of hut circles on Goonhilly Downs.

Hervan (SW6957 1645) lies just off the A3083 Lizard road at the entrance to Predannack Airfield. It leans sharply to the E, set in the hedge of a garden, and is extremely weather-worn and mis-shapen, though it does have a possible alignment to the Four Lanes/Carnkie stone row (see p.6) & the well on Carn Brea (see p.5)

OTHER SITES

WELLS - **St.Ruan's Well** (SW716 147) lies just over the hedge beside an old path that ran from Grade Church (which has a mysterious holed stone inside the church) to St.Ruan. It has a beautiful serpentine stone building enclosing a well of clear cold water.

Other holy wells (now destroyed) were at St.Keverne (SW790 214), Gunwalloe Church Cove (SW659 205), and Mathiana's Well (SW734 236) & Caervallack (SW730 246) both near St. Martin in Meneage.

CROSS STONE - **St.Rumon's Cross** (SW 7171 1510). Not far from St. Ruan's Well at Ruan Minor in a private garden is what appears to be a menhir that has been Christianised by having a cross carved in relief, a similar process to that at Mabe churchyard (see p.9).

CROSSES - **Cury Churchyard** (SW6780 2126). A 9'2" wheel-headed cross. **Predannack Cross** (SW6707 1704). A 5'6" cross in a field S of Mullion in a good state of preservation.
Trelanvean Cross (SW7514 1957). Reached by a path S of the B3293. Legend that the cross was thrown down by a man looking for gold, an indication that it may be on the site of an original menhir - also a number of alignments pass through.
Lizard Cross (SW7076 1262). A 4'6" cross used as a rubbing post and a gatepost, standing midway between the Church and Lizard point.

Grade Church (SW7120 1430). This church stands isolated from any settlement at the end of a green lane. The building replaces an earlier one that had several unusual features, including a north chapel and aisle, and a NW internment, hinting at pagan origins. In a corner inside the church is a curious holed stone, that may have originally marked the sacred site.

Poldowrian (SW7550 1690). This site lies between Cadgwith and Coverack. Traces of mesolithic and neolithic worked flint and tools have been found in this early settlement. There is a small museum here and it is open on special days during the year (see local press).

Trelan Bahow (SW7490 1955). A cist cemetery here revealed an Iron Age burial of a woman of high standing with jewellery and bronze hand-mirror embossed with Celtic design, which is now in the British Museum.

Church Cove (SW662 205). Gunwalloe Church Cove is the focus of many powerful lines of energy, that may be connected to the ancient sanctity of the place. Between the cliff and the church there was a Llan, an early religious site, and a Dark Age royal manor was located at Winnianton Farm. Grass-marked pottery and animal bones have been uncovered by the shifting sand dunes.

The Three Brothers of Grugith (SW7616 1978)Behind Zoar Garage on the B3293 amongst shrub and gorse lies the remains of what may have been an entrance grave or burial cist, though this has been disputed. There appears to be a ruined capstone and perhaps two other stones: the 'capstone' has shallow identations on it, which may be cup-marks or natural weathering. It does stand on a alignment between Crousa Common stones & TrelanveanX

ALIGNMENTS AND PATTERNS

LIZARD POINT (SW698 115). This is the most southerly point of Great Britain, and a place of much ancient mystery. From Lizard village a network of sunken lanes runs in all directions to the coast, with its hidden caves and rocks. One of these, known as Pistol Ogo (Cave of the Waterfall) lies beneath sloping ground known as Pistol Meadow. 50ft beyond this in a northerly direction lies a narrow-entranced but deep cave "The Giant's Cave" (SW6989 1154). Psychic researcher Andy Collins has discovered that from this cave a distinctive off-shore rock called "Man of War" is visible with its distictive rounded horns shape. On the left hand side of this rock the sun sets at midwinter solstice, an alignment that may well have been noticed and celebrated in former times.

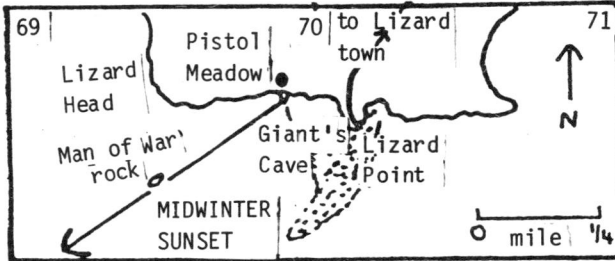

THE LIZARD LANDSCAPE ZODIAC It has been suggested by mystic Sheila Jeffries that there is a landscape zodiac of 12 signs, outlined by the ancient trackways, lanes, field patterns and stones of the Lizard peninsula, similar to the Glastonbury Zodiac. This is the ultimate ink-blob test — either you see it or you don't, but the shapes are indicated in the map below.

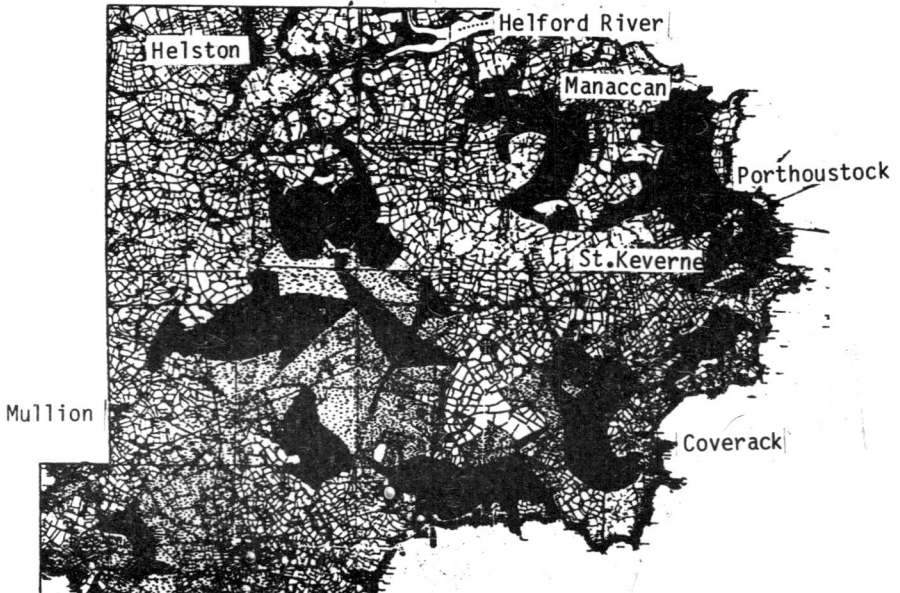

Correct to 10 metres width & +2^0 adjustment to true azimuth.

Grid ref.	Site	Offset
6590 3155	Longstone Down round barrow	4.067
6592 3154	Prospidnick menhir	−4.076
7526 2119	Drytree menhir	0.009

Grid bearing: 137^0 55' Length: 13962.06m.

7526 2119	Drytree menhir	−1.155
7461 3135	Eathorne menhir	1.913
7362 4694	Two Burrows round barrow	−0.758

Grid bearing: 176^0 21' Length: 25802.17m.

7171 3536	Stithians cupmarked stone	0.861
7777 2103	Tremenhir menhir	−0.280
6879 4227	Carn Brea north settlement	−0.581

Grid bearing: 157^0 4' Length: 7501.63m.

6957 1645	Hervan menhir	−0.028
6856 3940	Camkie stone row (?)	0.464
6859 4092	Giant's Well Carn Brea	−0.435

Grid bearing 177^0 42' Length: 24489.62m.

6831 3654	Nine Maidens south circle	1.015
6643 4072	Carn Brea west settlement	−9.474
7526 2119	Drytree menhir	−2.531

Grid bearing: 155^0 39' Length: 16876.546m.

7752 2009	Crousa Common menhir	0.006
7493 3794	Stithians Well	−1.743
7362 4694	Two Burrows round barrow	1.158

Grid bearing: 171^0 44' Length: 27131.76m.

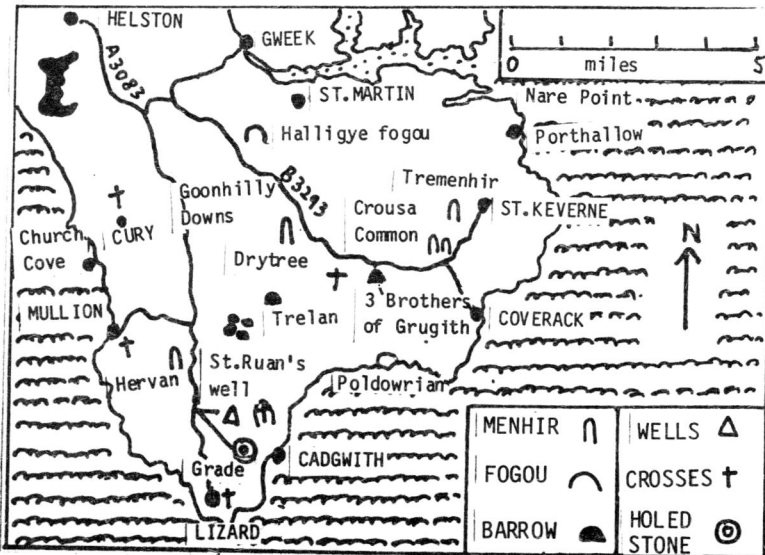

mid cornwall

Mid–Cornwall, running from the Fal estuary to the Fowey estuary on the south coast, and the cliffs of St.Agnes to the cliffs of Padstow on the north coast, is a land of much contrast. From the beautiful Roseland peninsula with its pretty wells and crosses and the historic land of King Gerent, it is but a few miles to the bizarre moon–landscape of St.Austell's china–clay works. Here on the downs that were dug up for the white mineral, were formerly standing stones put up by our ancestors who worshipped a different god. As we move eastwards we come to the lovely Fowey estuary, and the land of King Mark of Dumnonia, and also perhaps a hidden place of the Goddess. At the centre of the area lie several dramatic hill–forts and rocky outcrops, Helman Tor, Roche Rocks, Castle–an–Dinas, places of much ancient sanctity. And on the north coast, there are prehistoric settlements near Newquay, and a wonderful array of holy wells in some beautiful countryside, largely unknown and unvisited by the thousands of holidaymakers that throng the seaside resort every year.

Here we are in the heart of Cornwall, an area now bisected by the busy A30 route, which once would have been the main trackway across the top of Cornwall. From this centre, our Neolithic and Bronze Age ancestors came to occupy the hilltops and downs with their megalithic monuments; from here our Iron Age predecessors ruled over their kingdoms and queendoms, remembered in their legendary names and stories; from here the early Celtic saints came to built their oratories and the holy wells that sanctified the places of natural spiritual refreshment; and from here the seafarers from Ireland and Brittany made a route across the Saint's Way and through the centre of Cornwall herself at Lanivet. And here, we can still explore these hidden by–ways of Cornwall's past, and discover they remain alive today.

LANIVET – SACRED CENTRE OF CORNWALL

The idea of the Omphalos (literally "navel") as the sacred centre of a particular land or territory, has occured to many different cultures in different places, from Greece (Delphi), to Mecca, to England, which has several candidates. Every Celtic land also had its own centre: in Ireland it was the holy hill of Tara; in the Scottish Hebrides the sacred isle of Iona; on the Isle of Man Keeil Abban, a spot that stood right in the centre of a line between the most northerly and southerly points of the island crossed by the east–west axis.

Cornwall too has something similar. The centre of Cornwall is at Lanivet near Bodmin, in the churchyard. There is an old saying that the spot is "in the middle of the county, north and south, east and west". It is the mid–point on the Saint's Way, the route across Cornwall taken by the early Christian saints and travellers from Ireland to Brittany and back, which can still be walked today from Padstow on the north coast (13½ miles away) to Fowey on the south coast (also 13½ miles away). It is also about 50 miles from Land's End and 40 from the Tamar, making it symbolically "the geographical centre of Cornwall." It may also be much older: Lanivet literally means the church–site (Lan) at the pagan sacred place (Neved), an indication that the site had pre–Christian significance.

Later, this sacred site became Christianised, as many pagan places did, and there are two elaborately carved crosses in the churchyard. One is featured in the crosses section [p.37] but the other is especially interesting in this context because it is the Omphalos of Cornwall, marking the centre of the land. It stands behind the church in a cleared grassy area, and has the most decorated shaft of any wheel–cross in Cornwall. All 4 sides are covered with decoration, sub–divided into 6 panels by incised lines. Amongst the most interesting features there is a symbol of 2 concentric circles with a dot in the middle. Could this be a representation of the Omphalos itself? The motif recurs, this time with one concentric circle carved between the legs of a curious figure that looks as if it has a tail! Could this be a representation of the devil, an indication that here we have the pagan centre of the land? Other indications of Lanivet's pre–Christian significance can be found in the Feast Day, which is on the Sunday after the last Thursday in April – clearly the old pagan Celtic May festival of Beltane. Altogether, a very interesting sacred centre of Cornwall.

For locations of places mentioned see map on p.32.

tRistan & iseult countRy

The legend of Tristan and Iseult is one of the most enduring Cornish legends. First written down by the Breton jongleur Beroul in 1160 C.E, it is clearly based on an earlier Cornish telling of a legend that has been lost to us. Beroul tells a dramatic tale of illicit love, passion and pagan magic' set in a Cornwall that is still identifiable today. The early part of the tale when Tristan is at the court of King Mark seems to be set around the Fowey area [see p.31], but much of the latter part when the lovers are fleeing from Mark seems to take place in the lands around present-day Falmouth & Truro, although in a sense the geography of the tale is a mythic one not tied to any specific location. However, for anyone who wishes to follow the trail of the lovers, the Falmouth-Truro area provides some fruitful ideas.

MALPAS (SW845 528) or "the perilous ford". A few miles outside of Truro, this ancient crossing place of the river is still a quiet and secluded place. When Tristan & Iseult took refuge it was in the forest of Morrois or Moresk, which still remains today, though much reduced in size.

A track still leads along it to the ford where Iseult tricked Mark by being born across by Tristan disguised as a leper. There is even the site of a former leper colony near Malpas at Kiggon.

BLANCHELAND. Across the river from Malpas is the parish of St.Kea (SW844 417). In medieval times and earlier the area was referred to as Alba Landa or "Chyrgwin" in Cornish, the 'white land', so called perhaps because of the profusion of quartz stones in the soil there even today. This was the Blancheland where at Goodern (still the name of a meadow) Iseult had to come to Mark's Hunting Lodge for her trial. Close by is a large mound said to be the burial place of King Mark's predecessor, the pagan King Teudar who was killed in battle there. At Goodern in the 18th century a peasant unearthed some gold and silver treasure that made him a gentleman, while on the barrow midsummer bonfires were lit until recent times. In the nearby church of St.Kea, a tranquil spot situated in a creek of the Truro river, there is a curious smooth round-shafted stone, with a circular band carved on it. It may have been a pre-Christian stone that was adapted by having a cross-head fixed, but that has now long gone. This whole area is a place of much ancient sanctity and remoteness, though in Tristan and Iseult's time it was clearly an important royal centre.

For the sites of the Tristan Stone & King Mark's Castle see p.31.

kInG GeRent countRy

Moving south from Malpas & Old Kea we come to the Roseland peninsula a place of much gentle beauty. A little inland from the coast at Portscatho 'and Pednvadan Point (see below) is the village of Gerrans (SW873 352) named after King Gere.nt. According to the Anglo-Saxon Chronicle, he fought the Saxon kings Ina and Nun, and his seat of power was supposed to be nearby at **DINGEREIN CASTLE** (SW882 376), an Iron Age circular hillfort with two concentric ramparts, now split in two by ploughing. Gere.nt may have been named after a god of the underworld, who descended there and carried out a ritual sacrifice to renew the fertility of the land.

The story was probably later written in the early Welsh "Mabinogjan" as "Gere.nt, son of Erbin", a tale of Celtic pagan magic and shape-shifting.

The legend of his death is a strange tale of mythic significance. He is supposed to be buried under **CARNE BEACON** (SW913 387) at Veryan in a golden boat with silver oars in which he was ferried across Gerrans Bay. Carne Beacon is one of the largest Bronze Age barrows in Britain, some 107ft in diameter and 21ft high, containing a central stone cairn covering a large cist. Burial in boats or boat-shaped mounds is something associated mainly with Bronze-Age Scandinavian peoples, although the Anglo-Saxon epic "Beowulf" has a similar burial. We have here a very ancient legend that places Gere.pt in a mythological context to do with sun-gods and kings. It has been suggested [by Andy Norfolk in "Meyn Mamvro" 26] that if someone stood on Carne Beacon at dusk at mid-winter in the Bronze Age, they would have seen the dying sun/fertility god set over Pednvadan Point. If they had stood on Pednvadan Point at dawn at midsummer they would have seen the sun/fertility god rise renewed over Carne Beacon. When the sea was calm there would have been an impressive path of reflected light across Gerrans Bay. All this may help to explain the legend of the golden ship with silver oars.

ST. AUSTELL DOWNS

St. Austell Downs is a granite outcrop that has turned to China Clay, and has been extensively mined in recent times, leaving a strange lunar-like landscape. This means that, although the area would have been occupied from the Neolithic onwards (such as the hill-top enclosure on St. Stephen's Beacon) almost all traces of prehistoric remains have been obliterated. However a few standing stones do still remain.

At **Roche** (SW9867 6012) in front of some old people's bungalows stands an 8ft menhir, originally standing on LONGSTONE DOWNS (SW9838 5614) from where it was moved when threatened by china clay workings. During this move the top was broken off and put back on again and the crack can still be seen. Excavation showed that this stone originally replaced an earlier stone, which in turn had replaced an earlier wooden post, an interesting development of use.

Another curiously placed stone is **Mount Charles (Gwallon)** longstone (SX0296 5212) which stands in the grounds of penrice School in St. Austell (ask permission to view). This fine 11ft stone originally had another rounded stone near to it which may have been the capstone of a burial chamber, and there are also a number of barrows in the vicinity

A few miles to the north near Boscoppa is **Menear** (SX0345 5448), a 6½ft stone in a field with extensive views towards the Mount Charles site. It also seems aligned on to a far hill on the equinoxes, the shape of the top of the stone parallelling the shape of the hill itself. →

There were also possible former standing stones at Penstras (SW997620? & 998621?), and Tregonetha Downs (SW960626), and a stone row or stone circle at Nine Stones Common (SX010560?).

HOLY HILLTOPS

In the area of mid–Cornwall there are a number of enclosures, many on mounds and/or dramatic hilltop sites. Often these were constructed during the Iron Age, but some date back as early as the Neolithic. Their exact function is not known: they may have had a defensive role, but equally there is much evidence for peaceful occupation of living and working.

South of St.Austell near the village of Porthpean lies **CASTLE GOTHA** (SX0276 4964), an Iron Age site excavated in the early 1980s. Here were found traces of the huts of metalworkers, together with brooches and a linch pin in the form of a human head, which places it strongly in the Celtic tradition of venerating the human head.

To the west of St.Austell near St.Stephen–in–Brannel lies **RESUGGA CASTLE** (SX9400 5101), a well–preserved Iron Age fort in an attractive setting. Dowsers Paul Broadhurst and Hamish Miller felt that it was an important ritual centre where ancient ceremonies had once invoked the Earth Spirit at crucial times of the annual cycle. In nearby St.Stephen Church is displayed a descendant of the Glastonbury holy thorn.

North of St.Austell near the village of Roche is the extraordinary **ROCHE ROCK** (SW9910 5960), a granite outcrop rising over 100ft into the air. On the summit, built into the rock itself is an ancient chapel, dedicated to St.Michael, and originally the haunt of the Celtic saint St.Conan. It is

a powerfully impressive place, made even more mysterious by legend of a well at its base that is supposed to ebb and flow with the sea, though it is many miles inland. Solar and lunar energies meet here in this mystical place.

To the north–west of Roche across the A30 lies **CASTLE–AN–DINAS** (SW9460 6240), a large Iron Age hillfort some 850ft across. Huge earth ramparts enclose a settlement area that may include Bronze Age barrows. 1 mile west at Quoit (SW9232 6193) is the capstone of a destroyed dolmen **Devil's Coyt**.

Finally, to the east near Lanivet reached by minor roads lies **HELMAN TOR** (SX0680 6070), a rocky outcrop that may originally have contained a Neolithic hill fort, similar to Carn Brea near Redruth. (Neolithic greenstone axes have been found). It also continued into Bronze Age times, with a settlement on the western slopes. To the north–east lies a Neolithic dolmen **Lesquite Quoit** (SX0707 6276), which would have been similar to Carwynwen Quoit [mentioned on p.7]. Lesquite is now in a semi–ruined state, with a fallen capstone 17 x 9ft leaning against 6ft & 5½ft upright stones.

ST.BREOCK DOWNS

Full details of all these sites may be found in the N.Cornwall Guide.

To the NW of Castle-an-Dinas lies the moorland area of St.Breock Downs with an interconnected series of menhirs. In a field beside the A39 three miles NE of St.Columb Major lies **Nine Maidens stone row** (SW9363 6745) [pictured right], consisting of 9 stones, 6 of which are still standing. The row originally pointed to a 7ft standing stone, known as **The Fiddler** or **The Old Man** (SW9394 6820), which was broken up 100 years ago, leaving only a fragment. The Fiddler was also part of a group of standing stones forming an alignment across the Downs. To the E at the highest spot lies **Men Gurtha** (SW9678 6831), a 10ft high stone re-erected in 1956, weighing some 16.8 tons, the heaviest erected stone in Cornwall. Around its base was a layer of quartz stones. Half a mile to the E is **St.Breock Downs menhir** (SW9732 6825) some 7ft tall. Some miles to the W off the edge of the Downs is a 11ft white quartz menhir at **Music Water** (SW9056 6802), and further still to the SW is a 9ft stone at **Airfield** (SW8715 6802), re-erected in 1932. All these stones form a pattern of alignments, indicated in the map below. There is also a dolmen **Pawton Quoit** (SW9658 6960) with a massive capstone in a field to the north of the Downs.

Music Water

Men Gurtha

St.Breock Downs

Airfield

Music Water menhir 9056 6870

Men Gurtha re-erected at 9678 6831 50 yds

Boundary stone.

Airfield menhir 8715 6802

The Fiddler 9394 6820

Nine Maidens Stone Row

St.Breock Downs menhir 9732 6825

KING MARK COUNTRY

Marcus Cunomorus or King Mark was a legendary Cornish leader, mentioned in the early medieval Life of St.Samson. He appears to have ruled during the first half of the 6th century extensively in Cornwall and perhaps in Brittany too. Two sites to the north of Fowey are particularly associated with him, and with the Tristan and Iseult legend as well.

CASTLE DOR (SX1030 5480) lies beside the B3269 2 miles N of Fowey. It dates from the Iron Age, but legend attributes its use later at the time of King Mark. It consists of a circular enclosure, some 290ft across, surrounded by a bank and a ditch.

TRISTAN STONE (SX1112 5224). Also called the Longstone, this 9ft inscribed stone stands beside the A3082 road at the Four Turnings crossroads, about 1 mile NW of Fowey, and 1 mile S of Castle Dor. It too is associated with King Mark, as its inscription "Drvstanvs hic iacit Cvnomori filivs" has been translated as meaning "Tristan lies here, son of Cunomorus". The earliest record of the inscription (by Leland in the 16thC) also included the words (from a piece of the stone now perhaps broken off) "Cvm domina Clusilla" which may mean "and his wife Miranda", which may be a Latinised Greek word for the Cornish (I)Eselt. The stone stands near the southern end of the Saints Way from Padstow to Fowey.

The farm to the west of the Tristan Stone is named Lankelly, which is derived from lann = scared enclosure, and kelli = grove or copse, thus meaning "a sacred grove". In addition, the headland joined by Lovers Lane, running from here to the sea, is named St.Catherine's Point, Catherine being an anglicised pagan solar goddess. The chapel on the point, St.Katherine's Chapel could thus have been built on an earlier sacred site, a very suitable place for a sun–goddess site. The whole area has very sacred connotations.

31

NEWQUAY

This coastal area is covered with ancient barrows and two special sacred sites. **Trevelgue Head** cliff castle (SW8250 6310) is an outstanding Iron Age headland site to the N of Newquay Bay, excavated in 1939, containing barrows and cists that revealed a huge funeral pyre had burnt for several days before the barrow was covered. **Trethellan Farm** settlement (SW7980 6140) lies about 1 mile inland from the Gannel estuary, and was thoroughly excavated in 1987, when evidence was found of Bronze Age occupation, followed by re-use in the Iron Age as a cemetery with strong spiritual and ritual associations connecting with their former ancestors.

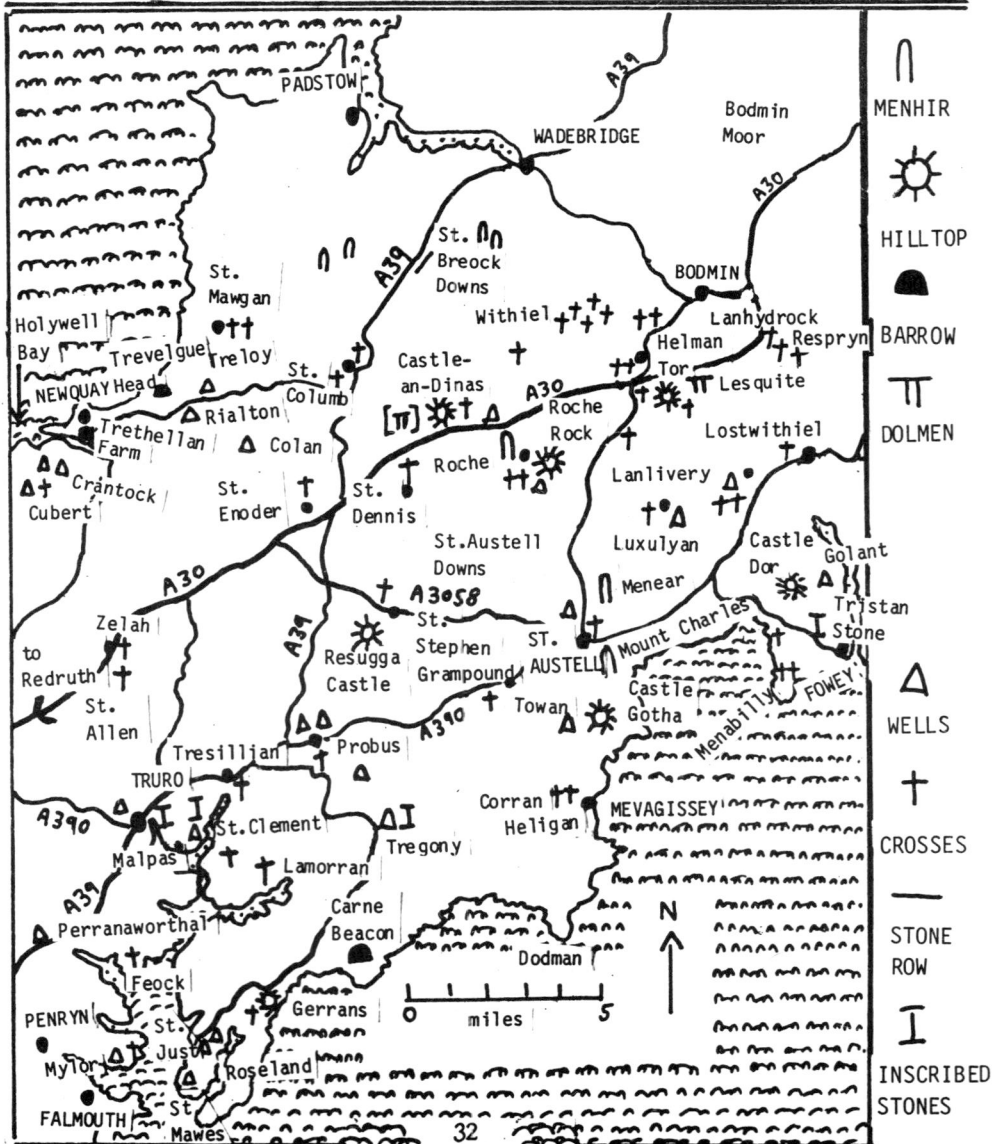

Map legend:
- MENHIR
- HILLTOP
- BARROW
- DOLMEN
- WELLS
- CROSSES
- STONE ROW
- INSCRIBED STONES

NEWQUAY. There are a number of beautiful wells nearby the town.

CRANTOCK. In this village there are 2 wells: the village holy well (SW789 609), with its curious beehive structure, dedicated to the saint who arrived from Ireland with his band of followers. ↓

St.Ambrusca's Well (SW789 609) is on the road going out towards the Gannell Ferry. It is locked but has has an interesting carved door. ↓

CUBERT (SW773 588). On Trevornick Farm holiday village across the sand dunes is this lovely well, restored in 1936, with multiple arches, an inner sanctum and much running water.

Cubert Well

HOLYWELL BAY (SW764 602). In a cave on the beach is an amazing and unique holy well in the calcalareous–coloured rock itself. Mothers formerly bought their sickly children here to be put through and healed.

COLAN – Lady of Nance Well (SW870 604). Down a track to the hamlet of Mountjoy, the well lies beside a stream. Renouned for the cure of sore eyes, and foretelling future.

RIALTON PRIORY (SW847 619). In the garden of the Priory at St.Columb Minor, this lovely well was (in 1840) removed to Somerset by the Steward who was then forced to return it! ↓

TRELOY (SW858 623). In a boggy wooded area on Treloy Farm (ask directions), a very peaceful and lovely setting for this restored well

PERRANAWORTHAL - St Piran's Well (SW779 388). On the A39 at the Norway Inn, a track runs up behind the inn, and on the right a pathway leads down to a beautiful grotto-like well. St. Piran is the patron saint of Cornwall, but this well lies a mile or so below the church, indicating the pre-Christian origins of the site.

MYLOR (SW820 353). This church beside the creek has a sun-symbol cross [see p.36], and a granite and slate holy well in the churchyard.

ST.JUST-IN-ROSELAND (SW849 358). Across the peaceful creek lies the enchanting church of St.Just, with a well in the churchyard. However, the actual holy well lies outside the church, through the lower lychgate and along a footpath, indicating its pre-Christian origins. St.Just was a son of Gereint, the ür-sun god [see p27].

ST.JUST LANE - Holy Well of Ventongassick (SW854 356). Beside the main road junction to St.Just Lane lies this deep well with steps leading down to the water.

ST.MAWES (SW847 332). At the side of the road above the Victory Inn this well was originally attached to an ancient chapel and shrine, but now stands rather forlornly with a locked entrance door.

KENWYN (SW819 458). This quiet and peaceful village lies just to the north of the busy metropolis of Truro. The well, which is older than the church, lies inside the church-yard, in a good state of repair, and is reached by steps.

TREGONY - St.Cuby's Well (SW928 450). This little-known and less-visited well lies at the end of a muddy land bordering on some fields running down from the Police Station. It is a hidden and secret-ive little well with overgrown veg-etation. St.Cuby was associated with Ireland, Angelsey,& the Isle of Aran.

ST.CLEMENT (SW853 438) This tiny village about 2mls E of Truro has a pretty little well on the banks of the Tresillian River. Meyrick suggested that the church here was pagan in origin, and the well one of the most ancient in Cornwall.

PROBUS. Golden Manor (SW923 468), Venton Glidder (SW901 495) & Tre-lowthas (SW885 472), now all ruined.

VICTORIA - St.Gundred's Well (SW985 617). A small lane north of the busy A30 leads to a cottage, behind which a steep path goes down to a wooded valley and this hidden holy well. A dark and secretive place.

GOLANT - St.Sampson's Well (SX121 551). A roofed stone well next to the porch of this peaceful church on the site of a 6thC hermits cell.

ST.AUSTELL. 2 miles S of the town on Towan farm (ask directions) is TOWAN WELL (SX015 489), a large stone building restored in 1937, which lies at the bottom of a field. ↘

MENACUDDLE (SX013 535). A mile to the north of St.Austell below the A391 Bodmin Road, this is a large 15thC building housing clear running water. Renowned for divination and good fortune. ↓

LUXULYAN – St.Cyors Well (SX054 580). At the bottom of the village next to the road is this 15thC granite building recently restored.

LANLIVERY – St.Bryvyth's Well (SX078 590). From the footpath beside the Inn, a track on the left leads through a hedge maze and around a picturesque marsh to this lovely secluded and beautifully-positioned well. A hidden delight.

INSCRIBED STONES

CUBERT (near Perranporth) (SW7861 5776). This stone is built into the west wall of the church tower. Its inscription reads CONETOCI FILI TEGERNOMALI = "Conetocus son of Tegernomalus", who may have been a 6th century Bishop.

CUBY (near Tregony, Truro) (SW9275 4527). This inscribed stone, dating from the 6th or 7thC, is built into the SW corner of the church. It reads NONNITA ERCILINI RIGATI... TRIS FILI ERCILINI, giving the names of the 3 children of Ercilinus.

ST.CLEMENT (near Truro) (SW8905 4386). In the churchyard is an inscribed stone from the early 6thC, originally found in a nearby field. It reads IGNIOC... VITALI FILI TORRICI. The original inscription meant "Vitalus son of Torricus", and was also oulined in ogham script. IGNIOC (possibly meaning Cunignus) was a later addition, and an even later change happened in the 7thC when the top of the stone was hollowed out to form a Celtic cross.

RIALTON (near Newquay). Originally at SW849 618, this stone was moved in 1991 to Truro Museum. The inscription reads (F)ILI TRIBVNI BONEMIMORI which refers to "the son of Tribunus", who was possibly the king who ruled at the time in Demetia (West Wales), from whence came many of the migrants who brought to Cornwall the fashion for the inscribed stones.

LOST/DESTROYED STANDING STONES
PROBUS – Tregeagle(SW864 469?) Manheirs Farm/Longstone Close (SW9294 4835) ST.DENNIS (SW9523 5778) & Enniscaven (SW9632 5944) STONE ROWS at Carsella(SW944 577?) & Pelgodu(SX0432 6207 – 0440 6199) close to Lesquite Quoit [see p.32].

PERRANZABULOE (SW7720 5646). Standing on Penhale sands, this 8ft 4-hole cross of St.Piran was first recorded in 960 C.E, the earliest reference to a stone cross in Cornwall. It stands a mile east of the reburied St.Piran's Oratory.

CUBERT CHURCHYARD (SW7862 5776). Known as the Ellenglaze Cross, it can be found on a granite shaft against the wall of the church.

ST.COLUMB MAJOR. 2 crosses here. 1)(SW91323 6238) Fourhole Cross in the churchyard, & 2)(SW9098 6066) in Black Cross village built into a recess in a garden wall beside the A39, the village taking its name from the black-painted Latin cross.

ST.MAWGAN IN PYDAR. 2 crosses. 1)(SW8725 6594) Bodrean Cross is a wheel-headed cross found in the churchyard. 2)(SW8723 6591) An intricately ornamented cross in the grounds of Lanherne convent.

ST.ALLEN CHURCHYARD(SW8225 5060) 3 crosses: A 6'3" wheel-headed wayside cross by the porch door, and 2 other small wheel-headed cross-heads in the churchyard.

TRESILLIAN (SW8702 4648). A cross-head outside the Holy Trinity church in the village.

ST.ENODER (SW8924 5694). A wheel-headed cross found beside a road then taken to the churchyard.

CASTLE-AN-DINAS (SW9574 6262). To the W of the hillfort [see p.29] on Tregonetha Downs is the 'Cross and Hand' or 'Crossy Ann', a wheel-headed boundary cross in an overgrown thicket.

WITHIEL (SW9931 6525). A 7½ft cross in the grounds of the Old Rectory.

MYLOR CHURCHTOWN (SW8201 3525). This cross is the tallest in Cornwall 17' 6", though nearly 7' is now buried in the ground. It is most unusual, having a pagan sun-symbol carved on both sides, and the church itself has recently uncovered 16thC mason's sigils carved around the door. Together with the well in the peaceful creek-side churchyard [see p.34], a most interesting place.

LAMORRAN CHURCHYARD(SW8787 4175) A tall slender cross, whose head was replaced in 1975.

ST.MICHAEL PENKIVEL (SW8556 4272) A Latin cross beside the road NW of the church leading down to Malpas [see p.26]. A former well (Fenton-gollan) lay to the N of here.

GERRANS CHURCHYARD (SW8728 3516). A 6' 8" wheel-headed cross, probably originally a wayside cross.

TREVALSA CROSS (SW8170 5183). Recently restored with a missing piece, this wheel-headed wayside cross stands on a roadside verge about ½ml E of the A30 at Zelah.

FEOCK CHURCHYARD (SW8391 3953). An excellently-crafted cross, very Celtic in appearance.

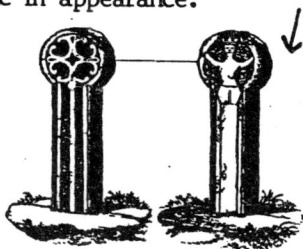

PROBUS (SW8857 4666). At the entrance to Trelowthas Farm on the A3078, a 4½ft incised cross.

CORRAN CROSS (SW9849 4570). Also known as Beacon Cross, a wheel-headed cross placed on the wall.

HELIGAN MANOR (SW9991 4646). A 8'3" wheel-headed wayside cross in the private grounds of Heligan.

GRAMPOUND (SW9556 4735). This cross-shaft standing beside the B3287 is now missing its head.

ST.DENNIS CHURCHYARD (SW9507 5828). This inscribed 8½ft cross stands in situ in the churchyard, which is on the pagan site of an Iron Age hillfort. It has been suggested that the inscriptions too are pagan, representing double-headed axes.

ROCHE. 2 crosses 1) Churchyard (SW9879 5978) A wheel-headed cross inscribed with dots, lines and a hilted sword! 2) Rectory Meadow (SW9876 5990). A 4' wheel-headed cross probably in its original site.

ST.STEPHEN IN BRANNEL CHURCHYARD (SW9450 5329). Wheel-headed head.
ST.AUSTELL CHURCHYARD (SX0143 5243). Small Latin cross.
MENABILLY. 2 crosses in the private grounds (SX 1025 5103 & 1022 5116)
TYWARDREATH (SX1008 5410) Damaged 4-holed cross at Trenython Hotel.

LANIVET. This area has many crosses In the churchyard (SX0396 6422) is the central cross of Cornwall [see p.25] and another 10½' elaborately carved one on the W side. Reperry Cross (SX0464 6331) stands at the junction of 6 ancient tracks a mile to the SE, and other crosses also once marked the ancient Saints Way, including St.Ingunger (SX0597 6334) & Fenton Pits (SX0610 6297). Other wayside crosses include Bodwannick (SX0371 6561), Lesquite (SX0665 6268), Treliggan (SX0557 6411), Laninval (SX0495 6566), Tremore (SX0208 6506), Woodley (SX0270 6395), and Lamorrick (SX0357 6460).

LOSTWITHIEL – Crewel Cross (SX0893 5909). A 9' restored cross at junction of B2269 & A390 roads.
1½mls E of the town is St Nighton's Cross (SX1284 5996) a wheel-headed cross cut from red granite standing in the yard of St.Nighton's Chapel. Waterlake Cross (SX1021 6340) is in a small cottage garden near Respryn.

LANHYDROCK. 3 crosses 1) churchyard (SX0851 6361) 2) Estate gardens (SX0852 6346) 3) Cemetery (SX0862 6417), originally beside Saints Way.
LUXULYAN. 2 crosses 1) churchyard (Three Stiles cross) (SX0521 5807) 2) Trevellan Cross at Lockengate on A391 (SX0319 6131), both crosses originally marking the ancient track from here to Bodmin.
LANLIVERY. 2 crosses 1) Trethew Cross on old church path (SX0735 5881) 2) Sandyway Cross (SX0791 5796), a wayside cross discovered in 1936 at the junction of 2 ancient lanes, then stolen in 1990 and subsequently recovered by police.

south east cornwall

From the Saints Way, crossing Cornwall from Padstow to Fowey, we move eastwards and southwards to the area south of Bodmin Moor. Here we begin to approach England, and the land takes on a different quality, the countryside more rolling and gentle, the place–names more Anglicised. Here in 838 C.E the last battle for Cornwall was fought and lost on Hingston Down (near Callington) when the Anglo–Saxon King Egbert defeated a Cornish army augmented by Danish Vikings. Before that, the area had been occupied in prehistoric times and there are traces of this in one stone circle, some (possible) standing stones, tumuli on the downs and hills, and a cliff castle. But much has been lost as agricultural clearance and more intensive farming took place in the area, and later, in the Tamar Valley, mining. There are also few Celtic crosses here, and those of a relatively later date.

But what the area does have are a number of wells, which have often been beautifully preserved. This may be because it was settled early, or was on Celtic migration routes across the River Tamar. Whatever the reason, these wells are a treasure and a joy to discover. Often hidden at the bottom of valleys, or in farms behind sleepy villages, or beside quiet country roads at the junction of old trackways, they are a pilgrimage to find and a pleasure to savour. It is water that runs through the veins of this area: the water of the streams and springs and wells, the sea that brought migrating people to and from the safe havens, and, perhaps most symbolically, the River Tamar herself (named after a nymph/Goddess Tamara) which marks the boundary of the ancient kingdom of Cornwall, and which the travellers of old would have to have forded. Here we can see the reason why Cornwall remained distinct and different for all those centuries, and why even today she still remains in many ways a separate and unique land.

DULOE STONE CIRCLE
(SX2359   5830).
Signposted off the road on the south side of Duloe village, the circle lies up a lane and then in the far side of a field. It was restored in 1860 when a bisecting hedge was removed from the site, and at least one urn was found.

It is a beautiful and utterly unique circle on several counts. It stands isolated away from any other circles in this part of SE Cornwall, it is only about 35ft in diameter, consisting of just 7 upright and one fallen stone, probably in their original positions, and the stones all consist of shining white quartz, a material that was known to be sacred to our ancestors. A key-stone at Boscawen-un stone circle in West Penwith is similarly made of quartz, and a bed of quartz stones has been found at other sites such as the Hurlers central stone circle on Bodmin Moor, but this is the only complete circle of quartz stones known. Quartz is supposed to have special healing qualities, and cows have been observed to go into the circle especially to give birth. A very special site indeed.

Although it is away from the sites of Bodmin Moor to the north it does align with some of them. This may be coincidental or deliberate.
(1) De Lank Quarry menhir (SX1000 7530) - Calvannack Tor stone row (middle at SX1288 7174) - Duloe stone circle. (2) Hurlers North (SX2584 7146), Central (SX2582 7139) & South (SX2580 7132) stone circles - Duloe circle.

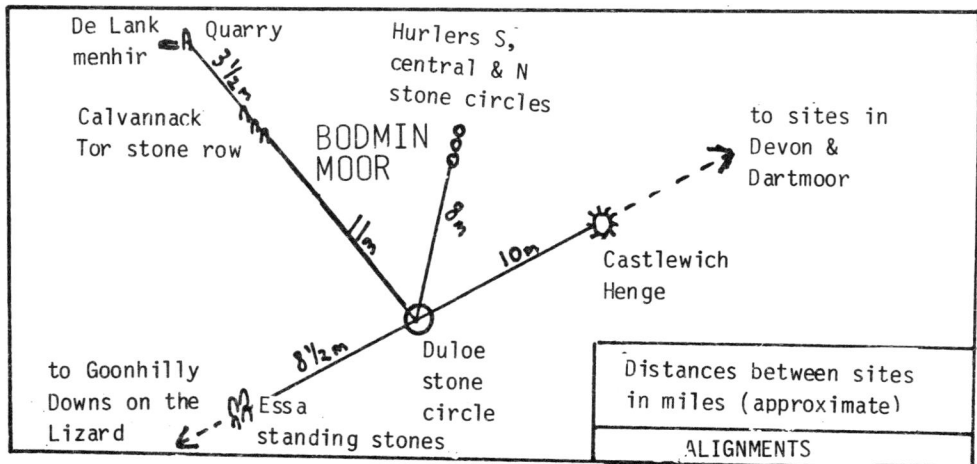

De Lank Quarry menhir
Hurlers S, central & N stone circles
Calvannack Tor stone row
BODMIN MOOR
to sites in Devon & Dartmoor
3½m
10m
Castlewich Henge
8½m
Duloe stone circle
to Goonhilly Downs on the Lizard
Essa standing stones

Distances between sites in miles (approximate)

ALIGNMENTS

ESSA STANDING STONES. In the fields above Polruan-by-Fowey are 10 curious standing stones, which seem to form a group. At SX1380 5128 are 5 stones, which have been shifted: one is the Devil Stone, used for resting coffins and now lying on the grass verge; two more lie on the verge outside a gate; & another pair are built into the hedge inside the gate. At 1377 5110 and 1372 5098 (photo right) are 2 standing; at 1383 5104 is the base of one; and at 1380 5128 are 2 more (formerly at ap.138 510) lying on the grass verge.

These stones may originally have formed a significant pattern, but as they have been moved it is now impossible to tell. However, a ley line does run through the complex from Goonhilly Downs in the Lizard (with many tumuli), Essa stones, and on to Duloe stone circle, Castlewich Henge [see p.41], and across other bridges and crossroads into Devon and Dartmoor.

Two other stones formerly stood in Polruan at ap.SX128 509, one 4-5ft high, but were bulldozed for a housing development.

THE GIANT'S HEDGE (SX141 572 to 247 536). This linear earthwork originally ran some 8 miles from Lerryn to Lanreath and Looe, although now only sections remain. It may have formed the northern boundary of an Iron-Age kingdom. Enclosed within it are the Bake Rings (SX187 549), a settlement enclosure, and Hall Rings (SX214 555), a hill fort, both near Pelynt and dating from the same period.

PELYNT ROUND BARROWS (SX200 544). From the earlier Bronze Age period, this is a group of 10 round barrows. One barrow yielded a dagger that may have come from Mycenaean Greece, dated to 1710-1495 BCE, important for showing trading links from/to Cornwall at this early period.

LOOE ISLAND (SX255 505). (Privately owned but day trips from Looe). Looe Island, also known as St.George's Island, or St.Michael's Island has evidence of a Bronze Age urn burial, and later a Celtic monastic settlement. There are the ruins of a chapel there, connected with the ruins of a small chapel above Hannifore on the mainland, both owned by Glastonbury at one time.

LOSTWITHIEL CHURCH (SX104 593). To the north of Fowey/Polruan lies the town of Lostwithiel, with a unique font, more pagan than Christian, with powerfully-carved symbols, including a 'Green Man' with a Bishop's Hat, and a grotesque gargoyle with serpents entwining about its projecting forehead.

CALLINGTON AREA

About 10 miles east of Bodmin Moor lies the area of Hingston Downs and Callington. Here prehistoric peoples also lived, and, despite later mining activity, their remains still cover the landscape. To the south-west of Callington, there is CADSON BURY (SX3430 6740), an Iron Age causewayed camp enclosure, and to the south-east lies VIVERDON DOWN (SX3810 6745) with several tumuli. Closer to Callington (about a mile to the south-east from the town) is CASTLEWICH HENGE (SX3707 6853), with Neolithic bank and internal ditch. It appears that henges were some kind of ritual sites, and there is one on Bodmin Moor (Stripple Stones) which contains a stone circle. Castlewich Henge has an outcrop of greenstone nearby, used in the manufacture of Neolithic ritual axes, which archaeologist John Barnatt has suggested may have been a similar kind of sacred hill site. It aligns to Bodmin Moor with the Hurlers South stone circle (SX2580 7132) & De Lank Quarry menhir (SX1000 7530), and various cairns and Craddock Moor menhir (SX2390 7113).

Just to the north of Callington lies the granite outcrop of KIT HILL, occupied by Neolithic/Bronze Age peoples, who built several tumuli here. There is also an earth-fast stone atanding on the NW side of the hill (SX3728 7203) below the Quarry dumps. It is made of granite with a high proportion of quartz, and is nearly 7ft high with a base 5ft long and 3½ft wide. It is difficult to find, being surrounded by undergrowth and is not in a conspicuous position. Although a natural rock outcrop, it may well have been venerated by ancient peoples and seems to form two alignments:-

[1] to a tumulus on Kit Hill (SX3750 7070) - tumulus on Viverdon Down (SX3810 6745) [2] another tumulus on Kit Hill (SX3737 7067) - Dupath Well.

In addition, John Barrett has dowsed the area and has found a number of energy lines crossing the hill and running through some Bronze Age barrows and enclosures [see "Kit Hill - Our Hill" booklet by Ann Eade).

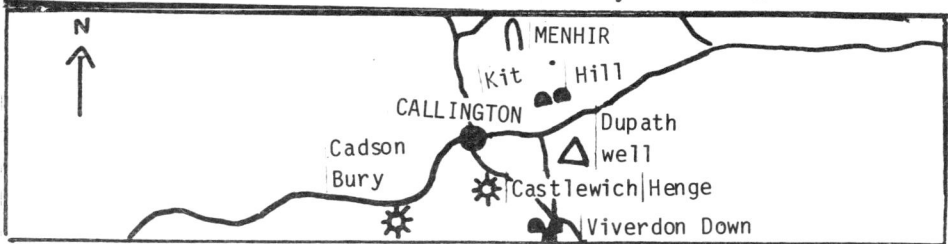

About 7 or 8 miles north of Kit Hill approaching Launceston, Greystone Bridge crosses the River Tamar on the border between Cornwall & Devon. Here at Longstone Farm (SX362 803) near a quarry there was formerly a stone row of 3 head–height stones, destroyed a few years ago.

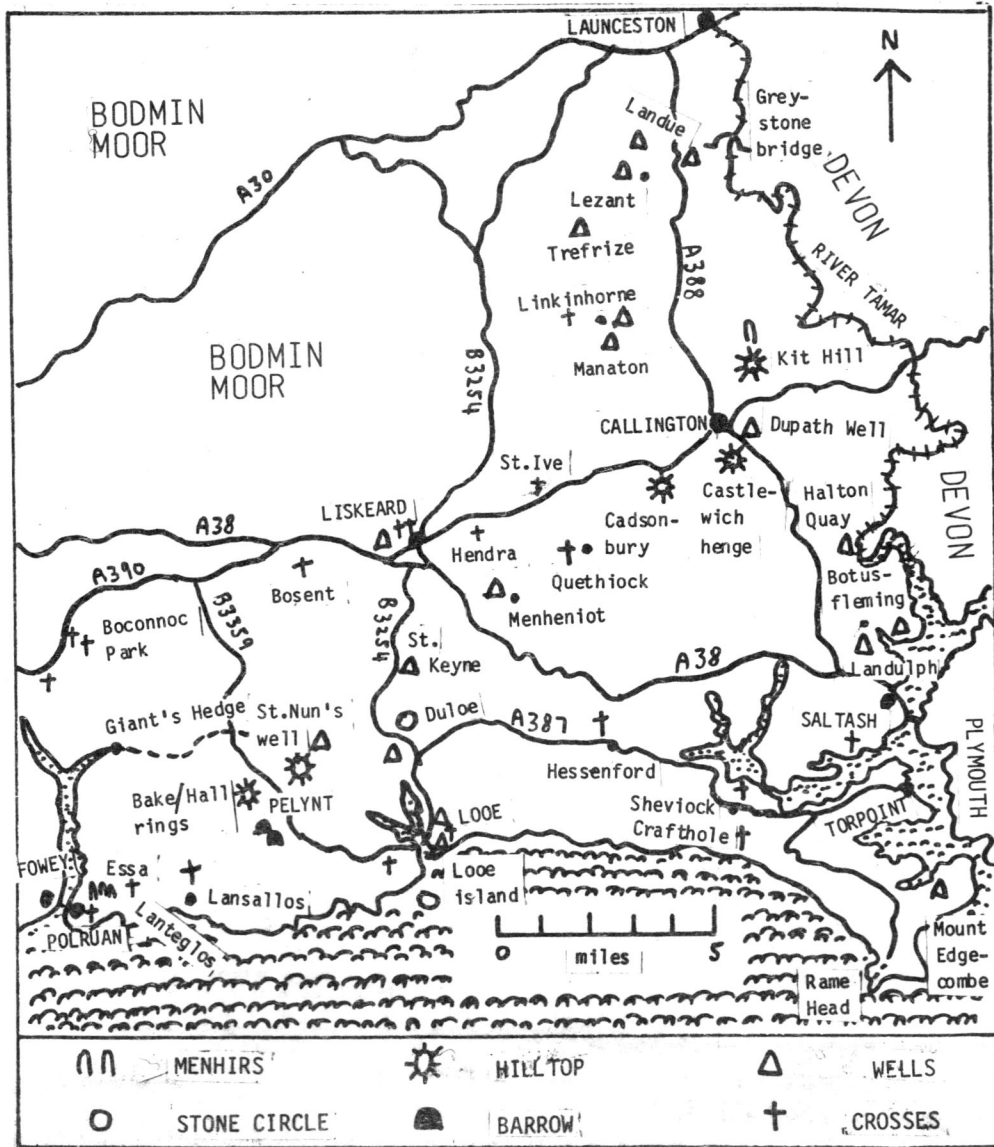

BODMIN MOOR

A30

BODMIN MOOR

A388

B3254

LAUNCESTON

N

Landue

Lezant

Trefrize

Linkinhorne

Manaton

Greystone bridge

DEVON

RIVER TAMAR

Kit Hill

CALLINGTON

Dupath Well

St.Ive

Cadson-bury

Castle-wich henge

Halton Quay

DEVON

LISKEARD

A38

Hendra

Quethiock

Menheniot

Botus-fleming

A390

A38

Bosent

St. Keyne

Landulph

B3359

Boconnoc Park

B3254

St. Nun's well

Duloe

A387

Hessenford

SALTASH

Giant's Hedge

PLYMOUTH

Bake Hall rings

PELYNT

LOOE

Sheviock Crafthole

TORPOINT

FOWEY

Essa

Lansallos

Looe island

POLRUAN

Lanteglos

miles

0   5

Rame Head

Mount Edge-combe

∩∩ MENHIRS	☀ HILLTOP	△ WELLS
O STONE CIRCLE	🔴 BARROW	✝ CROSSES

42

CROSSES OF EAST CORNWALL

BOCONNOC PARK. This private estate E of Lostwithiel has 2 crosses, both removed from Lanlivery in the 1840s. Druids Hill (SX1265 6127) has been elaborately remounted; Boconnoc (SX1422 6060) is a 7' high cross, with some curious carvings on the shaft.

LISKEARD. 2 crosses in St.Martin's Churchyard: the Culverland Cross (SX2539 6441) a 4½ft Latin cross, & Tencreek Cross (SX2542 6433) a 6'10" Latin wayside cross.

ST.IVE (SX3096 6715). 2 crosses in churchyard One 5½' Latin cross, the other a small wheel-headed one.

LINKINHORNE (SX2943 7484). A 3ft Latin cross in the grounds of Northcombe Farm, visible from road

QUETHIOCK CHURCHYARD (SX3134 6472) A 13½'high cross, the second tallest in Cornwall, with intricate ornamentation, much of which has now disappeared. It was discovered in 1882 broken in 4 gateway parts

MENHENIOT (SX2684 6553). A recently-discovered wheel-headed wayside cross re-erected at Hendra Farm next to a public footpath.

LANTEGLOS CHURCHYARD (SX1448 5150) A 4½ft Latin cross, the head of which was discovered half buried in the mud at Pont Pill Creek!

POLRUAN CROSS (SX1276 5073) Also called St.Saviour's it stands beside the road leading into the village.

LOOE. The Tregoad Farm cross is now housed in the E.Looe Guildhall Museum (SX2555 5335). The Parlooe Cross (SX2461 5288) stands in a hedge recess 1½mls SW of the town

LANSALLOS CHURCHYARD (SX1720 5158). A 3' Latin cross originally found on the churchpath from Lanteglos to Lansallos, and subsequently placed in the churchyard. It has a deep depression in the top of the head, perhaps used for libations

CARRACAWN nr Hessenford (SX3220 5736) A 5'10" Latin cross set into a hedge on an ancient route to Devon

TREMATON,nr Saltash (SX4045 5821) A small 2'3" cross with a deep depression at the top of the head, similar to Lansallos churchyard.

CRAFTHOLE (SX3650 5421) Probably the market cross - a 3' high Latin cross with the top limb missing, mounted on a base.

SHEVIOCK (SX3629 5504). Known as the Stump Cross this 7' Latin cross was positioned at a crossroads connected with the Old Pilgrims Way between Polbathick & Crafthole Junction with the ancient Cremyll-Lands End route. After 1945 it was removed, a base made for it, and re-erected on top of the hedge at the corner of a field at Cross Farm.

BOSENT CROSS (SX2225 6355) Where minor roads cross near St.Pinnock is a 5'8" semi-Gothic Latin cross.

43

LISKEARD & LOOE AREA

LISKEARD – St.Martin's Well [Pipewell] (SX252 645). In centre of town below the street and behind a locked gate – the water is now condemned! Once well visited for healing and favourable marriage prospects for women.

MENHENIOT – Holy Well (SX289 628). In centre of village outside wall of vicarage near the church. A stone and roofed structure.

ST.KEYNE – Holy Well (SX248 603). Found 1 mile SE of St.Keyne Church at a crossroads, in a sunken lane beside the road. Restored in 1932, it is a beautiful well with clear running water, and St.Keyne herself reputedly planted an oak, an ash and an elm here. Whichever newlywed drinks first of the waters, man or wife, will be the ruler of the marriage, a legend that can also be found on St.Michael's Mount, which the saint was also reputed to have visited. ↓

LOOE – 2 holy wells: St Marys in the town (SX256 534) nicely restored but with a padlocked gate; and St Martins (SX258 542) on the Sunrising Estate, now fenced off since a tragic accident in 1992 in which a young toddler fell in the well and was drowned.

DULOE – St.Cuby's Well (SX241 579). About a mile SE of the stone circle beside the road to Sandplace lies this well in a good state of preservation with an ancient well-building enclosing a seat and an inner well with clear water. A former granite basin carved with figures of dolphins and a griffin was removed to Duloe church. ↓

PELYNT – St.Nun's Well (SX224 564). In valley of West Looe river, steps lead down a path to a site of great mystery and deep tranquility. The well-building is surrounded by oak and thorn trees, and contains an ancient bowl into which the water drips. Many strange legends assoc-iated with it, including a guardian elf, a curse on removing the bowl, and piskies who would follow anyone home who did not leave an offering ↙

NORTH OF CALLINGTON

LEZANT – This area abounds in holy wells, and was an early religious monastry and settlement, the name meaning "holy place". The presence of the wells may have been the reason that the place became sanctified by the early Christian church.

St.Michael's Well (SX337 792). On the left 100yds north of Lezant church is this small stone building with clear water. St.Michael as a saint often replaced an earlier pagan god/dess.

St.Lawrence's Well (SX337 798). About ½mile north of Lezant church the well lies behind a house but is now in a concrete cistern. The remains of a chapel are also here.

St.Bridget's Well (SX350 796). This well is on the private estate at Landue, where there was also a chapel to St.Bridget. The saint is the Christianised version of the pagan goddess Bride, who was probably brought from Ireland to Cornwall by early traders and settlers. The well is very hidden amongst trees and beautifully kept with clear running water. ↓

TREFRIZE – All Hallows Well (SX312 769). Reached by a path from the 16th Century farmhouse at Higher Trefrize (ask permission) in a field below the garden of Lower Trefrize house. A reconstructed well house encloses clear water that is still piped to the farmhouse.

LINKINHORNE – St.Melor's Well (SW319 732). From the village church take the road to Browda and ask at the first farm on the left on whose land the well stands in the corner of a boggy field. The wellhouse is attractive and its situation pretty, but the well much less so. Water is drained out so it is now virtually dry, and contains debris dumped from the farm. However, an interesting legend involves St. Melor's beheading by his uncle: the severed head speaks and commands that it be set on a staff in the ground, from where it is transformed into a beautiful tree from which comes a fountain of water. A legend that probably goes back to Celtic pagan times. ↓

MANATON – Holy Well (?) (SX337 720). In garden of the Manor House under a large holly tree. Old stone and roofed building.

Details of CARADON (SX291 714) & LEWANNICK (SX274 807) wells may be found in the "EM Guide to Bodmin Moor & North Cornwall" booklet.

CALLINGTON – Dupath Well (SX374 693). Below Dupath Farm outside Callington. The most impressive well structure in Cornwall, and now in the care of English Heritage, who have provided a plaque saying it is a pre–Christian shrine. A 16thC granite chapel with turrets encloses the water which is fed through a stone trough. A legend is associated here about a duel fought between a poor knight Colan and a rich man Gottlieb for the hand of a maiden, which has echoes of ancient mystery about the lords of summer and winter fighting over the Goddess of spring and the Land, Sovereignity. ↓

HALTON QUAY – St.Indract's Well (SX417 659). At the bottom of a track from Chapel Farm on the left is a stone and roofed building with an attractive wrought–iron gate (locked) and a statue of the Virgin Mary in the back. The well was restored and re–dedicated in 1951, but unfortunately, despite this, the water has now been drained off for secular use. Nevertheless, the well is in a remote and peaceful setting on the banks of the River Tamar looking across to Devon.

BOTUSFLEMING – Holy Well (SX405 614). Another well in a nearby village (on the corner next to the old school) with a statue of the Virgin Mary (and dedicated to her). An old stone building in good state, but again gate is locked. ✓

LANDULPH – Holy Well (SX428 614). The well is in marshy boggy land on the edge of Kingsmill Lake and is also overgrown with thorn and brambles! Very difficult to find.

MOUNT EDGECUMBE – St.Julian's Well (SX447 521). This is the easternmost well in Cornwall, approaching the border at Plymouth Sound. It stands on a wooded bank beside the road to the Cremyll ferry, and is in good condition, having been restored by the Earl of Edgecumbe in 1882. It would have been the first well encountered by pilgrims as they crossed from England into Cornwall.

And finally....   <u>**RAME HEAD**</u>

Rame Head (SX418 484) is the furthest south-eastern point overlooking Plymouth Sound and Devon. Almost completely detached from the rest of the mainland, Rame Head was probably settled first by the Neolithic peoples who built a Chambered Tomb (now destroyed) at SX4183 5090, and then by Iron Age peoples who built a cliff castle here. Later the place was sanctified by the building of a tiny chapel in 1397 C.E, 21ft by 9ft with walls 3ft thick, dedicated to St.Michael, showing it was built on an earlier pagan site. It is now quite ruined but stands impressively on the conical-shaped headland, looking very similar to other sacred sites such as Glastonbury Tor and Brentor. It also has a very interesting alignment. Its axis is orientated towards the Mewstones, another conical rock outcrop that is visible some 5 miles away out to sea, and on September 29th each year (which is St. Michael's Day, and close to the Autumn Equinox) the sun rises over the Mewstones when viewed from the Chapel. This is a dramatic example of the continuity of pagan megalithic alignments into Christian times, and a living geomantic symbol of the sacred interrelationship of the earth and cosmos, microcosm and macrocosm linked together at the moment of first light.

<u>CONCLUSION</u>

At Rame Head we come to the eastern borders of Cornwall with Devon,having travelled nearly 100 miles from Trencrom Hill and St.Michael's Mount in west Cornwall. The two island/peninsula hilltop sites of St.Michael's Mount and Rame Head are both linked together by being dedicated to St.Michael, and the other hilltop sites along the way were also sacred to our Neolithic and Iron-Age ancestors. They mark the highspots on the land, the focal points for the people's connection with the sun gods and goddesses of the cosmos. Many of the sites built by the megalithic peoples, and also natural rocky outcrops, were deliberately aligned to significant solar and lunar events as people connected with the deities and spirits of the universe. The goddess of healing and spiritual nourishment could also be found in the holy wells, many of which still remain today in beautiful and secluded settings through-out Cornwall, and the early Christian inscribed stones and crosses show a continuity with the sanctity of the past. All these places throughout mid-Cornwall from the west to the east can still be visited and enjoyed, places of peace and beauty among the hustle and bustle of 20/21st century life. There is still much of Cornwall that is hidden or little-known, and waiting to be discovered afresh by those who love and cherish the ancient land.

BIBLIOGRAPHY AND FURTHER READING

GENERAL
Barnatt, John - Prehistoric Cornwall (Turnstone, 1982)
Cornish Archaeology   (Cornwall Archaeological Society)
Meyn Mamvro   (Meyn Mamvro Publications)
Miller, H & Broadhurst, P - The Sun & the Serpent (Pendragon, 1989)
Weatherhill, Craig - Cornovia (Alison Hodge, 1985)

Tangye, Michael - Carn Brea (Dyllansow Truran, 1981)

CROSSES
Blight, J.T - Ancient Crosses & Antiquities of West Cornwall (1856)
            - Ancient Crosses & Antiquities of East Cornwall (1858)
Henderson, Mary - Survey of Ancient Crosses in Cornwall (MS, 1985)
Langdon, A.G - Old Cornish Crosses (1896, reprinted Cornwall Books 1988)
Langdon, Andrew - Stone Crosses in Mid Cornwall (Old Cornwall, 1994)
Langdon, Andrew - Stone Crosses in East Cornwall (Old Cornwall, 1996)
Rowe, Laura - Granite Crosses of West Cornwall (Bradford Barton, 1973)

WELLS
Broadhurst, Paul - Secret Shrines (Pendragon, 1988)
Lane-Davies, A - Holy Wells of Cornwall (Old Cornwall, 1970)
Meyrick, J - A Pilgrim's Guide to the Holy Wells of Cornwall (1982)
Quiller-Couch, M & L - Ancient and Holy Wells of Cornwall (1894, rep.1994)

INSCRIBED STONES
Thomas, Charles - Guide to Inscribed Stones (Meyn Mamvro nos.19 & 20)
Thomas, Charles - And Shall These Mute Stones Speak? (Univ.of Wales, 1994)

ALSO AVAILABLE

EARTH MYSTERIES GUIDES - Comprehensive illustrated guides to the alignments, ley paths and anomalous energies at ancient and sacred sites in Cornwall and Scilly.

The Earth Mysteries Guide to ANCIENT SITES IN WEST PENWITH
52 pages covering Stone Circles, Standing Stones, Holes Stones & Stone Rows, Cromlechs & Entrance Graves, Holy Hills, Fogous, Wells and Crosses.
Meyn Mamvro Publications, 1992/1993. SBN:0 9518859 0 1. £3.50.

The Earth Mysteries Guide to BODMIN MOOR & NORTH CORNWALL (including Tintagel). 48 pages covering Bodmin Moor, St.Breock Downs, Callington area, Stowe's Hill, Tintagel and Dark Age Cornwall.
Meyn Mamvro Publications, 1993/1995. SBN:0 9518859 1 X. £3.50.

The Earth Mysteries Guide to ANCIENT SITES ON THE ISLES OF SCILLY
36 pages covering all the islands plus The Ritual Landscape, The Arthurian Connection and the Lost Land of Lyonnesse.
Meyn Mamvro Publications, 1995. SBN: 0 9518859 3 6. £2.95.